MADAM *Belle*

MADAM
Belle

Sex, Money, and Influence in a Southern Brothel

MARYJEAN WALL

UNIVERSITY PRESS OF KENTUCKY

Copyright © 2014 by The University Press of Kentucky

Scholarly publisher for the Commonwealth,
serving Bellarmine University, Berea College, Centre College of Kentucky,
Eastern Kentucky University, The Filson Historical Society, Georgetown
College, Kentucky Historical Society, Kentucky State University,
Morehead State University, Murray State University, Northern Kentucky
University, Transylvania University, University of Kentucky, University of
Louisville, and Western Kentucky University.

Editorial and Sales Offices: The University Press of Kentucky
663 South Limestone Street, Lexington, Kentucky 40508-4008
www.kentuckypress.com

Cataloging-in-Publication data is available from the Library of Congress.

978-0-8131-4706-2 (hardcover : alk. paper)
978-0-8131-4707-9 (epub)
978-0-8131-4708-6 (pdf)

This book is printed on acid-free paper meeting
the requirements of the American National Standard
for Permanence in Paper for Printed Library Materials.

Manufactured in the United States of America.

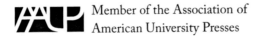 Member of the Association of
American University Presses

Contents

Illustrations follow page 102

Preface

Lexington, Kentucky, has entertained a long-running "infatuation" with Belle Brezing, as historian Thomas D. Clark once wrote.[1] Sadly, we do not know a lot about this notorious brothel keeper. She was not a woman for keeping a diary. Nor did she give interviews. Secrecy was a moral code in her sequestered world of prostitution, although the trade operated openly in Lexington in the neighborhood surrounding Megowan Street (now Eastern Avenue) in downtown's east end.

Nonetheless, what we do know about Belle is important to our historical understanding. She is a window through which we are able to view several salient aspects of the Lexington of her time, which, not unlike most American cities during the Victorian era and the early twentieth century, tolerated the presence of prostitution by corralling the brothels into designated "red-light" districts. Belle's life is a glimpse into public morals in Lexington and a case study of how concepts of morality—and the city of Lexington—changed over time.

This book is not solely Belle's biography. In fact, the reader will quickly discover that Belle disappears at intervals throughout the narrative. This occurs partly because of the scarcity of information about this fascinating woman. The other reason is that this book also concerns the times in which Belle lived. We cannot know Belle without knowing Lexington as she knew it. Much of her world was connected in some way to horse racing and breeding. A greater proportion of Lexington's population "spoke horse" in Belle's day than is true of modern times. The community's economy was intimately entwined with the horse business. Central Kentucky was horse country, and Belle's clients were horsemen.

Most of the information we have about Belle Brezing comes from the papers of E. I. "Buddy" Thompson, housed in Special Collections, University of Kentucky Libraries. Thompson acquired much of this collection from two Lexington men, Skeets Meadors and Joe Jordan, who collected photos and interviewed persons who knew Belle. Without their historical contribution, we would know even less about Belle. Meadors and Jordan also raided Belle's trashcans to retrieve account pages from her ledgers as well as photos and checks she wrote. Though much of this treasure trove had been torn by the time it hit the trash, these items add to our partial picture of Belle's life.

Also integral to preserving what we have of Belle's story were the Book Thieves, a group of collectors and local historians. While making a professional call during the latter 1930s to inspect Belle's books, they did what book thieves do: one of their members stole an account ledger. They also viewed a photo in Belle's album that gave us the year of her brothel's grand opening. I have searched but cannot locate the original ledger; nor has anyone found the photo. However, Thompson copied many of the ledger pages, and these copies are in his collection. I have to wonder why not all the pages made it into the collection.

Thompson also photocopied notations about Belle's burial site from records at Calvary Cemetery in Lexington. I was greatly disappointed that a spokesperson for the Diocese of Lexington failed to cooperate with my request to see the original records. As a historian, I would have liked to take my own look at these records, just as I took a fresh look at the rest of Thompson's collection.

I began researching Belle during the 1970s. I interviewed a handful of persons who remembered her, but these were older men who had grown up in an era when such things were not discussed with a young woman. As a result, my interview notes were sparse. I did, however, acquire photos. I also researched Belle's property records and her divorce proceedings as well as papers relating to the divorce of her mother and stepfather. I located her marriage license. I researched tax records. I found her listed in city directories. I researched the indictments against her, and I read Fayette Grand Jury reports that pleaded with the city to abolish the red-light district in Lexington. I assembled a partial picture of Belle, but not enough to write a book. Nor did I have the $500 that the family of Joe Jordan or Skeets Meadors (after all these years, I cannot recall which one) was asking for the Meadors and Jordan collection. I was an undergraduate at that time, and $500 seemed like a fortune. Even as I was winning the Philo Bennett Award in the University of Kentucky's Department of History for research papers I wrote on Belle in 1972, Thompson acquired the Meadors and Jordan box of documents.

I am thankful now that he did. Thompson produced a better book than I could have at the time, titling it *Madam Belle Brezing*. I did not feel ready to write Belle's story until after obtaining a doctorate in history in 2010 at the University of Kentucky. This degree, along with my knowledge about horse racing acquired through a long career as a sportswriter for the *Lexington Herald-Leader*, enabled me to take a different look at the documents Thompson had collected, which his estate donated to Special Collections at the University of Kentucky. I began to see Belle's life in a slightly different way than he had.

The historian's job is to read documents in a different way than they might have been read previously. For example, I saw connections to horse racing that Thompson had not recognized, particularly Belle's fondness for the sport. My interpretation of Belle's life placed her more central to horse racing. I also came to see her as less the prostitute with the golden heart (Thompson's view) and more a businesswoman keen on amassing real estate and wealth.

The more I studied Belle's life, the more I felt sorry for her true love, Billy Mabon. He is the tragic character of this narrative. Belle repeatedly cast him out of her house whenever the moneyman from the wealthy Singerly family arrived in Lexington. William and George Singerly, both from Philadelphia, reached into the Bluegrass to obtain trotting horses. We do not know which one of the two—or perhaps it was both—befriended Belle and set her up in her mansion. George's name appears in a handwritten notation in the Thompson collection. In Thompson's book, William appears without mention of George. I will leave it to readers to make up their own minds on the Singerly question.

The reader might wonder why Belle's story largely ends with World War I. The reason, again, is lack of information. We know most about Belle during the height of her career, from approximately 1890 to 1917. After she closed her business during the war, she became a semirecluse. We know almost nothing more about Belle until her death at age eighty in 1940. If policewoman Margaret Egbert and the Book Thieves had not made their separate visits to Belle's house in the 1920s and 1930s, respectively, we would know even less.

One final thought concerns the spelling of Belle's surname. People have spelled it every way imaginable, from Breezing to Breazing. I have chosen "Brezing" because that is the way her stepfather, George Brezing, spelled his surname. I find it ironic that for all her fame, Belle was cursed with a community unable to spell her name.

My hope is that some future historian will discover additional documents about Belle's life to enhance the historical record. As Clark wrote, Lexington has always been and probably always will remain fascinated with this woman—and for good reason. She is an intriguing character. More, she continues to tell us much about the city of Lexington, and about how deeply rooted every facet of the community was in horse racing and breeding. Belle was very much a part of all of this.

chapter **ONE**

The Elegant Miss Belle

A foggy twilight slid into Bluegrass horse country in the slipstream of a dreary day. May 14, 1890, had been eventful in one aspect only. Some seventy miles to the west, at Churchill Downs in Louisville, a racetrack drying out from heavy rains the night before had led to a mild surprise in the Kentucky Derby. The favorite, Robespierre, lost to a horse with the Irish name Riley. The news flashed out of Louisville in a flurry of Morse code, flying in bursts of static down the telegraph lines connecting Louisville with Lexington. The news was good for a Lexington woman named Belle Brezing as she opened for business that gloomy night. A Derby upset meant her clients would argue the outcome over more beer and bourbon than she usually sold. She knew, because she had been in this business a long time, that the liquor would be flowing until well past dawn. The customary cast of characters settled into her parlor, waiting for Belle to open her accounts ledger and thus signal the opening of the bar. As the spirits flowed like a rushing stream, Miss Belle kept score of the beverages dispensed. She settled in for a long evening and smiled at her guests, most of whom she counted as friends.

She was a pretty woman, not strikingly beautiful but pleasing in appearance. She stood only five feet two. What she lacked in physical stature, however, she made up for with a powerful presence. This petite woman, her rust-colored hair drawn tightly in a bun, had stood down whores and criminals, politicians and policemen while operating the most lavish and expensive brothel in the Bluegrass. Her friends included governors and former governors. Men in a wide array of powerful positions had befriended her: well-known bankers, lawyers, businessmen, and dealmakers in the horse business. They made the laws. They ran the local economy. And they had made Belle their confidante. She seemed to them the perfect southern belle, knowing precisely how to charm a man with a flicker of her eyelashes. Men had always liked Belle. She had few women friends.

Born and reared in Lexington, Belle had worked her way up the hierarchy of prostitution before opening her own brothel on North Upper Street near the city center in 1881. During those nine years, Belle had established her formidable client list. Most of her patrons were connected to horses because most of the powerful men in the Bluegrass were involved in some way in the business of producing fast and stylish bloodstock. You could hardly walk in the door of any business in Lexington without hearing "horse talk" and realizing that each and every business served the community's equine interests. The depth of this connection extended well beyond the hay and grain suppliers, saddle and harness makers, veterinary surgeons, dealers in horses, and other ancillary operations necessary for maintaining a large-scale livestock-breeding region. Bankers were heavily invested in the business, for they enlarged their banks' portfolios with loans to horse breeders. Numerous elected officials also bred bloodstock, thus ensuring that the racing and breeding of horses received favorable political treatment. Lexington's horse interests would even finance the construction of their own place of worship, the Episcopal Church of the Good Shepherd, raising nearly $200,000 beginning in 1924. In Lexington, horse culture was so bound up in the community that young boys grew up reciting horse pedigrees. As General George Armstrong Custer would note on a visit to the city in 1871, the talk in Lexington was nothing but "horse, horse, horse."[1]

Most people who frequented Belle's house talked horses as well, including Belle, who loved going to the races and betting on horses. She might have been quite successful at the racetrack, for in her position she certainly stood to receive privileged information from her clients. Belle's patrons knew she appreciated the horse business. They knew that, at her house, they could enjoy a night of drinking among like-minded men while perhaps sealing a deal on a horse. And if they so desired, they could walk upstairs for a longer night with one of Belle's prostitutes.

Men respected Belle's rules. They wore evening dress when they paid a visit to her place. Likewise, Belle did not permit her prostitutes to be seen downstairs unless they were wearing evening gowns. Men paid well for the privileges of Belle's well-run brothel. Hers was a $5 house in a neighborhood of $2 establishments—though liquor tabs ran an evening's expenses much higher.

On this Derby night, Belle was close to sealing a deal that would change her life considerably. In two weeks, she would file the property deed for a new house she had purchased a half dozen blocks to the east at 59 Megowan Street, now Eastern Avenue. (Belle also owned rental property, houses on East Fourth, Kent, and Dewees streets.) The house at no. 59 Megowan, assessed in 1891 at $4,000, would turn out to be the vehicle that propelled Belle from popularity into legend. Men would speak about Belle Brezing from as far away as Argentina. And it was all thanks to horses: the horse business had brought numerous horsemen to her North Upper Street address, among them the wealthy Philadelphian who gave her the money to purchase her new house.[2]

Belle bought 59 Megowan Street from Michael and Mary Foley. He was a grocer and landlord who owned six properties on Megowan Street, ten on Dewees Street, and two on Race Street, all in neighborhoods that bordered the racecourse for Thoroughbreds known as the Kentucky Association track. Race Street had existed as a racially mixed neighborhood since the end of the Civil War in 1865. Dewees Street, parallel to Race, formed part of a neighborhood that African Americans had populated since emancipation. They had come to Lexington to find jobs and escape white supremacists who fomented violence throughout rural areas in the postwar years. Megowan Street stood at the center of this black neighborhood. The famous African American jockey Isaac Murphy, who had ridden Riley to victory in that 1890 Derby, lived on Megowan Street for four years. But Murphy, who also won the 1884 and 1891 Kentucky Derbies, had moved a few blocks away in 1887 to a mansion on East Third Street.[3]

About the time Murphy moved, Megowan and the surrounding streets began transforming to a red-light district. Similar areas appeared in nearly every U.S. city during the Victorian era, as the notion of segregating prostitution to informally defined spaces became the social norm. Megowan, Wilson, and Dewees streets formed the nexus of Lexington's red-light district. Railroad tracks at Megowan Street's southern end below Main Street made a convenient boundary, making the area seem physically detached from the spaces "decent folk" frequented. Moreover, you had to climb somewhat of an incline to access Lexington's red-light district, which people began to refer to as the Hill.

Yet another reason this neighborhood seemed particularly suited to brothels was that African Americans comprised the major demographic. Lacking a voice in municipal government, black residents were unlikely to complain if city authorities paid little attention to immoral activities in their neighborhood.

Belle paid Foley $1,400 for the Megowan Street house, a two-and-a-half-story residence with eight rooms. Under Belle's direction, remodeling expanded the house to contain at least twenty rooms, and five years later, after a fire, she would add a third floor, bringing the number of rooms to twenty-seven. The expanded residence included a kitchen and a room for parties in the basement.[4] At least four chimneys rose from the roof, adding a sense of imposing scale to the remodeled house. Five steps led to a lattice entrance; a similar entrance stood at the side of the house, on the southwest corner of Wilson Street, inside a small yard fenced in iron. After remodeling, Belle's house may have been the largest on the street.

She threw open her doors officially in 1891 with a gala that was quite a social occasion. Musicians played discreetly behind potted palms in the style of the day. Electric lights, still new in Lexington, illuminated the parlor. An elegantly appointed table, extending the length of three adjoining parlors, held fine linens, silverware, cut glass, china, and American Beauty roses set in tall vases, a scene captured in a photo that attorney and local historian William H. Townsend viewed on a professional visit to Belle's house many decades later. Belle had inscribed on the photo, "My Opening Night, 1891." Beautiful prostitutes, dressed in evening gowns, sat at the table. The men in the photo also wore formal attire—and many of them were well-known leaders of Lexington society and business. Lexington had never seen a house of ill repute so plush, so lavish, and so elegantly furnished. No. 59 Megowan Street became a destination befitting the urbane Victorian gentleman's sense of order and style.

But the opening night gala still lay in the future on that Derby night of 1890. Belle served drinks and managed her girls as she did every night, including Christmas. Her customers were men who knew the family trees of horses by heart. They cited pedigrees of horses with a confident knowledge that generally led to commentary on the faults or strengths of each branch in the tree. They knew the family lines of horses as well as they knew their own family lines—along with those of everyone else in the small community that Lexington was then. The talk this night was of the Derby winner.

Discussion also may have turned to Riley's owner, Ed Corrigan, lately from Chicago. Corrigan, both a rogue and a man of wealth, fascinated others, even if few felt comfortable in his presence. He was as Irish as the name he gave Riley. Born near Montreal, Quebec, he grew up in Leavenworth, Kansas, where his family had moved in 1860. Corrigan began life with nothing. One of his first jobs was driving a horse-drawn hack. He worked his way up on construction gangs attached to the railroads and eventually made a fortune in the railroad business. Like any wealthy man in this Gilded Age of excess, Corrigan displayed his wealth with ostentatious trappings, including a large and highly successful racing stable. Racing patrons and rival sportsmen alike knew Corrigan's horses to be formidable competitors. He had the best jockey in the nation under contract—Isaac Murphy. The African American had named his own terms in agreeing to ride for Corrigan.

Corrigan crossed paths at the racetracks with the leading men of the turf, yet he never acquired the veneer of respectability that usually accompanied a man of his station. In fact, he possessed a violent temper, which often made the newspapers. He killed a sports editor in Kansas City, Missouri, in 1887. In Chicago, he fractured a man's skull with a heavy stick. He decked a couple of touts at Chicago's West Side racetrack, which he owned. At Hawthorne Park, a track he built, he threatened a few board members with his pistol. Like most industrialists, he hated organized labor. He dealt with a threatened strike at Hawthorne by knocking the union leaders cold with his fists.[5]

The men at Belle's house likely discussed Corrigan that night just as racing men throughout the United States talked about him. Some of these Bluegrass men had probably encountered Corrigan at racetracks before, and eventually they would interact with him locally, when he purchased a farm in Lexington around 1903. As long as they were making money in deals with Corrigan, Bluegrass horsemen would have suffered his ungentlemanly behavior. But when Corrigan eventually fell on hard times, no one felt sorry for him. In 1896, one newspaper took note of Corrigan's precipitous fall to financial ruin with this headline: "Ed Corrigan, Once Famous on the Turf, Now Carries His Dinner Pail."[6]

Liking the races as she did, Belle would have delighted in these and other stories. One of the regulars at her house, a youth of seventeen, might have had some personal stories to tell about Corrigan. Ernest Featherstone, though young, was already a man about town, steeped in horse culture and destined for a career as an international horse dealer. He favored trotters, although his budding interests also lay in Thoroughbreds. Featherstone knew everyone and everything going on in the horse business. Even at seventeen, he was immensely popular. Over the years, Featherstone would become one of Belle Brezing's most faithful customers and closest friends.

His presence at Belle's house at such a young age was not as unusual as it might seem. A visit to Megowan Street served as a Bluegrass rite of passage for some young men from good families. For example, Colonel Jack Chinn sent his son, Phil, to Belle's house for indoctrination into the mysteries of manhood. Featherstone and Phil Chinn differed from most who passed through Belle's front door in that later in life, both spoke freely about patronizing the brothel. They were not in the least shy about their history with Belle. This seems remarkable, considering both were men of standing in Lexington. Both developed successful careers in the horse business, becoming the go-to men to make a deal. Featherstone put together major deals with trotting horses while Chinn specialized in Thoroughbreds.

At age thirty, in 1903, Featherstone assembled a huge trainload of 114 trotters to send to Chicago. He had been exporting trotters from Lexington to Austria since 1897 and to Germany since 1898.[7] When he was not making the rounds of Bluegrass farms or hanging about the trotting track or the Phoenix Hotel, Featherstone could be found at Belle Brezing's house. He was especially fond and respectful of Belle's housekeeper, Pearl Hughes. Featherstone often told a story about Pearl and Belle salvaging a horse deal he might have lost but for them. According to Featherstone, he was preparing to depart no. 59 Megowan Street late one night when Pearl and Belle insisted he stay. He'd had too much to drink, and the women feared he might fall victim to thieves or worse—Megowan Street was crime ridden, typical of any red-light district. Aside from her concern for his safety, Belle could not afford the bad publicity that would result if something happened to Featherstone. But Featherstone insisted he had to go home. He needed to be fresh and wide-awake in the morning because he had to be at the trotting track. He had a big deal pending. Pearl promised Featherstone he could sleep in a room by himself so he would be well rested for his business the next morning. Pearl kept insisting, and Featherstone finally relented. He spent a restful night under Belle's roof.

The next morning, Pearl awakened Featherstone at 5:00, dosing him with a couple cups of coffee and a shot of whiskey. To his pleasant surprise, Pearl had prepared a hearty breakfast. She had brushed his clothes and shined his shoes. She also had called for a cab, and the horse and carriage were waiting outside the house when Featherstone was ready to leave. The hack got him across town to the trotting track on South Broadway in time to persuade his client to buy the horse he was selling. Featherstone always told his friends he had Pearl to thank for getting this deal done. Horsemen knew they could count on full service at Belle's.[8]

Phil Chinn related one venture he made to Belle Brezing's place. His father had invited the young man and some friends to dinner one night at the Phoenix Hotel. After dinner, the older man gave each of the youths some money and told them to go up to the red-light district. "Megowan Street is about four blocks from here," he said, and the young men understood this reference to Belle's. "You go on up there and if you don't get what you want there, go around on Wilson Street and get it. And if I ever hear of any one of you insulting a decent girl, I'll kill you, including you Phil, even if you are my son."[9]

Chinn, born in 1875, was two years younger than Featherstone. He came from a folksy background; his father was fond of spouting useful rural maxims such as "Never kill a red fox or vote the Republican ticket."[10] The elder Chinn won the Kentucky Derby in 1883 with a horse named Leonatus. His son, brought up in horse culture, matured into a clever broker who knew how to get the edge in any horse deal. Locals were fond of telling how Phil Chinn once paid a visit in the dark to the Kentucky Association track with chicanery in mind. He moved the pole marking the final quarter mile of the course closer to the finish line. He wanted the horse he was selling to work in fast time for a prospective buyer, which it would if the final quarter mile was a lot shorter than it seemed. The next morning, the horse did work exceedingly fast. Chinn sold the horse on the spot.

This was Belle's world—a world with the horse at its center, a world of gamblers and financiers, of bankers, politicians, and lawyers who by their Bluegrass birthright made their living from the horse. Years of listening to the conversations of these men had taught Belle much about fast horses. The horse world had enabled her rise from the streets. Trotters and Thoroughbreds would be named for her.

On Riley's Derby night, Belle gave every impression of a confident woman with her career on the rise. She could congratulate herself on making friends in high places. With the help of at least one friend in the horse world, Belle now had the financial means to operate her larger, grander house. Belle's intuition was right: no. 59 Megowan Street held the promise of a turning point in her career. She couldn't know, however, that this house would transport her into the realm of historical legend. Yes, she had come far, and this house would take her farther. In the quaint politeness of the southern style, men no longer called her Belle Brezing. They referred to her, most respectfully, as Miss Belle.

chapter TWO

Civil War and Home War

Belle Brezing's rise to madam of a prominent brothel was remarkable. Given the circumstances of her youth, she was fortunate to have succeeded at anything. Abandoned by her father, left an orphan at fifteen upon her mother's death, and lacking any means of supporting her newborn child, Belle was looking at a bleak future when she turned to prostitution as a teenager. Later, she revealed she had tried to kill herself—twice.

Belle was a child of the Civil War years. She was ten months old when Fort Sumter, South Carolina, fell to the Confederates on April 13, 1861. This incident set off four years of fighting that would deeply affect the Bluegrass. The scars of war would shape Belle's world. People in Lexington had long debated the inevitability of a civil war. For some time before Fort Sumter fell, differences of opinion raged over the southern question. Would the slaveholding states secede from the United States? Should Kentucky join them or stay in the Union? Words would fly and so would fists in the many saloons throughout the Bluegrass. Sarah Ann Cocks, Belle's mother, drank her way through a number of them.[1]

Belle's mother was single when she had the baby she named Mary Belle Cocks. The birth took place while Sarah lived in a rented house on Rose Street. The road intersected with Main Street and lay close by the city's eastern limits, convenient for Sarah's paramour, a farm worker. Elias Cocks was not Sarah's husband, although the two shared the same surname. They might have been related, for Sarah appears to have lived for a time with Elias Cocks's family in Woodford County. After the death of Elias's father, John Cocks, in 1848, Elias (thirty-five years her senior) and Sarah moved to Lexington. Six years before Belle was born, Sarah had given birth to another girl, Hester. Belle's birth marked a major turn in Sarah's life, for Elias disappeared shortly afterward. Sarah now faced life alone with two young girls to feed.[2]

Sarah Ann Cocks was an enterprising woman. Before long she had met and married another man, George Brezing. The marriage took place December 16, 1861, when little Mary Belle was eighteen months old. Brezing was a German immigrant who had arrived in Lexington a short time earlier. His marriage to Sarah was grounded in the saloon culture ubiquitous on downtown street corners. The two operated a beer saloon on Water Street.

Later George, Sarah, and the two girls had moved to West Main Street, near Jefferson Street, where Brezing opened a grocery. Operating a grocery may have seemed a tamer life than running a saloon, but Brezing, a violent man, began to frighten away his customers. He beat his wife both in private and public. He consumed large amounts of alcohol. "I have seen Mr. Brezing drinking . . . several times," policeman Thomas Webster reported.[3]

Brezing was not the only drinker in the family. Sarah could match her husband glass for glass, and their drinking bouts frequently led to fights. Neighbors and customers at the grocery began to avoid the family. One customer, Bettie Coons, happened upon the Brezings in the middle of a fight one day. Coons walked into the store just as George was throwing a bottle at Sarah. Coons fled in fear.[4]

Brezing paid John Millburn $200 annually to rent the grocery and the family's living quarters. But Millburn said later that he regretted having rented to his drunken tenant. He had one word to describe George Brezing: vicious. Millburn said he had seen George hit Sarah with such force he knocked her into the scales the couple used for weighing meat and produce. Following an unnamed difficulty with George, Millburn ended their business relationship. Brezing removed to the other side of Main Street, where he opened another grocery.[5]

Neighbors began to speculate about which one of the two, Sarah or George, would outdo the other with the bottle. The carousing did not stop at the new grocery. Brezing frequented houses of ill repute, not bothering to return home at night. Sarah began to spend her evenings picking up men in those saloons, which stood on nearly every street corner. Sometimes she brought men home with her, even though her two girls were in the house. But despite all Hester and Belle saw and heard, they remained loyal to their mother. Hester, thirteen years old when Sarah sued George for divorce, took her mother's side in the court proceedings, describing how Brezing would strike her mother with his fists—or whatever he could grab to throw at her. "I have seen him hit my mother with a chair. I have seen him draw a knife on my mother. It was a butcher knife. I saw him draw a pistol on her," young Hester stated while a clerk recorded her testimony with pen put to paper. Hester said Brezing was always drunk when he attacked Sarah. He broke the furniture, once smashing a bureau, a table, and some chairs with his hands.[6]

In addition to the domestic turmoil they suffered, Hester and Belle were growing up in troubled times. Three months before Sarah's marriage to Brezing, Union troops some fifteen hundred strong arrived in Lexington. The soldiers set up camp at the fairgrounds, now the northern edge of the University of Kentucky campus. Trotting races had been held at these fairgrounds since 1859, but the arrival of the soldiers put an end to racing—they used all the racetrack fencing for firewood. One Lexington resident wrote dispiritedly, "Our trotting track has been occupied by soldiers all the year and as the fencing has been burned, it is now an open lot." There were sometimes clashes between soldiers and Lexington residents.[7]

The Civil War turned Lexington into contested territory, with soldiers on both sides roaming the city. Union soldiers camped on the courthouse square alongside Main Street and Cheapside, site of the old slave market. They camped south of the city. They camped in Gratz Park, north of the city center. Now and again, Confederate soldiers rode through the city or made camp in Lexington. Moreover, many an opportunist outlaw passed through town with a pistol in his belt.

Residents walked cautiously among the armed visitors; you never knew what might happen on Lexington's streets. In September 1861, Union soldiers walking past the Phoenix Hotel on Main Street came under fire, the shots originating from an upper window of the hotel. Witnesses suspected Confederate sympathizers. Within minutes, Union infantry and cavalry arrived to search the hotel, bringing artillery with them. They failed to find the shooter. But they warned the inn-keeper that if such an incident happened again, the army would burn the hotel. This was the Lexington of Belle and Hester's childhood.[8]

Whether George and Sarah sided with the South or North is unknown. The two had so many personal problems, they may not have cared about larger events. Perhaps they did not even hold political views. But they could not have failed to notice the movement of soldiers, the increasing amount of theft occurring in the city, and the declining public morale as the conflict wore on.

Troop movements in and out of Lexington had been taking place since within a week of the war's onset. Among the first to march through town were armed men bearing the Confederate flag passing through on their way south. Some folks cheered these men on their way through the city streets. They shouted and invoked the name of Jefferson Davis, former student at Lexington's Transylvania University and now president of the Confederate States of America. Others watched with heavy hearts, saddened and even horrified at this treasonous march.[9]

By mid-May 1861, a month before Belle's first birthday, shipments of muskets sent from federal authorities began arriving in Lexington. Southerners mockingly called these muskets "Lincoln guns," a slur that bespoke their hatred for President Abraham Lincoln. Confederate supporters desperately wanted to get their hands on these weapons. Union sympathizers organized into Home Guards to defend their homes and city against invasion. One prominent citizen, David A. Sayre, stored a shipment of rifles and revolvers in his bank at Mill and Short streets to dole out to Home Guards. All the while, southern sympathizers grew more vocal, calling for Kentucky to secede.[10]

Unionists were worried about southern sympathizers in their midst, especially since it was impossible to know who was a rebel sympathizer. They could be neighbors. They could be friends. Confederate loyalists mixed freely with Unionists on Lexington streets. Families split over mixed loyalties. Many more could not make up their minds about which side to support. Kentucky was conflicted, angry, and uncertain throughout the war.

As a slaveholding state, Kentucky might have followed the southern slave states into the new Confederacy. But this did not happen, much to the relief of President Lincoln. He famously warned that "to lose Kentucky was to lose the whole game." More than anyone in Washington, Lincoln recognized the strategic value of Kentucky, straddling as it did the Ohio River between North and South. In the beginning, Kentucky attempted to stay out of the war, remaining neutral for the first three months of the fighting. But when incursions into the state by both armies made neutrality no longer possible, Kentucky officially stayed in the Union. Still, Kentuckians were a divided people, sending sons to the armies of both North and South. Throughout the war and even afterward, Kentucky wore a mask of shifting identities that no one completely understood.

The Brezings would have seen Union and Confederate sympathizers drilling for home defense on public lots or riding down Main Street past their grocery. Armies of both North and South camped in Lexington for varying periods; Union troops eventually declared martial law. Confederate guerrillas (men who served as partisan rangers, or army irregulars, tasked with fighting behind enemy lines) also rode through Lexington.

Frances Peter, daughter of a renowned physician, watched much of this activity from her family's home fronting Gratz Park, a pleasant square. Soldiers frequently camped in Gratz Park right outside Peter's front door. They often asked residents for rations for themselves and their horses. Peter found the Union soldiers polite and grateful for handouts. "But the chivalry [southern officers] expect to be taken into the best parlor & have everybody in the house waiting on them no matter how dirty & slovenly they may be," Peter wrote in her diary with ill-disguised contempt.[11]

The Brezings managed to keep their grocery in business despite frightening the neighbors. But then, soldiers made good customers and plenty of them passed by. One day in July 1862, an alarming rumor spread from the east end of Lexington to the west end, where the little grocery stood: John Hunt Morgan and his band of guerrilla fighters were riding toward the city. Morgan was a Confederate partisan ranger, born in Alabama and raised in Lexington, across Gratz Park from where Frances Peter lived. Early in the war, Morgan had slipped out of Lexington with his band of men to join the Confederate army. By early July 1862, he was "darting all around Lexington, burning bridges and army stores and capturing home-guards, and demoralizing the Union citizens."[12] Basil Duke, great-nephew of Chief Justice John Marshall, was Morgan's second-in-command. Among other loyal followers of Morgan was John B. Castleman, a horseman born into a major land-holding family north of Lexington on the Ironworks Pike. Castleman raised a company of forty-one men, which had joined with Morgan in time for this July 1862 raid.

Word of the impending raid reached the ears of the military commander of Kentucky assigned to Louisville. He promptly telegraphed the mayor of Cincinnati: "Send artillery to Lexington and as many men as possible by special train without delay." Cincinnati authorities replied by telegraph: "Five hundred men go tonight from here—great excitement everywhere." Meantime, the Union commander in charge of Lexington, Brigadier General William T. Ward, placed Lexington under martial law and issued this order: "All able-bodied citizens of Lexington and Fayette County report themselves at the courthouse square forthwith. Those having arms will bring them; those having none will be armed."[13]

Historian J. Winston Coleman Jr. described the scene: "A thousand horses were hastily impressed for mounted duty; all tippling houses and grog shops were closed; merchants boarded up their doors and all Southern sympathizers were ordered off the streets and to their homes. . . . President Lincoln, having received exaggerated reports of Morgan's strength, wired the Union commander, General Henry Wager Halleck: 'They are having a stampede in Kentucky. Please look to it.'"[14]

The Home Brigades had drilled for a week in anticipation of the raid. Stores closed early in the afternoons so that proprietors and clerks could report to the Home Guards for drills. "The blockade has been in force here for a week," the Reverend William M. Pratt wrote on July 20, "and no persons save the military are permitted to pass on the streets without a pass from the military authorities, or to go out of town. Soldiers and Cincinnati police patrolling the streets."[15] Everyone waited breathlessly for the raid—and it never happened. Morgan learned that Lexington was heavily protected and chose to keep his riders west of Lexington.

Less than two months later, Confederate general Kirby Smith defeated the Federals at Richmond. Lexington residents first heard about the outcome of this battle early in the morning. By sundown, all manner of refugees from the battlefield were pouring into Lexington. Coleman wrote that these included "panic-stricken [Union] soldiers, broken cavalry outfits, shouting and cursing officers trying to rally their men, many of whom . . . were deserting and slipping off to their homes north of the Ohio River." To add to this noisy confusion, Lexington residents learned that the Union army had decided to abandon Lexington.[16]

The Union troops smashed their store of guns and supplies so the enemy could not confiscate and make use of them. Bank officials and the postmaster emptied their buildings of contents and sent them away for safekeeping. "Every thought of saving the capital of the Bluegrass was abandoned," Coleman wrote. "With the clatter of hoofs and screeching locomotives the Federals evacuated the city."[17] Union sympathizers left behind feared for their fate.

Two days later, on Tuesday, September 2, 1862, about eleven thousand Confederate army soldiers under Smith's command poured into Lexington along the Richmond and Tates Creek roads. People heard bands playing and saw the Confederate colors flying as the southern troops arrived. Confederate supporters turned out in the streets to welcome these soldiers with boisterous cheers. Within another two days, General Morgan arrived. He led a brigade of eleven hundred men. They rode their horses up to Cheapside, the site of the slave market adjacent to the courthouse. There they dismounted. One of their first tasks was to open recruiting offices. To their surprise, not many in Lexington signed up.[18]

The Confederate occupation of Lexington did not last even a month. Two days before the Union victory at Perryville on October 8, 1862, the Confederates abandoned the city. Morgan moved elements of his command to Bryantsville, covering the retreat of the Confederates following the loss at Perryville, and then he sought and received permission to return to Lexington. Early on October 18, he and his men engaged two battalions of Ohio cavalry in a battle at the Henry Clay estate, Ashland. Confederates were taking prisoners on the grounds when they came under friendly fire. It was a crazy, mixed-up scene.[19]

As the war wore on, Peter could see people around her losing their sense of right and wrong. She wrote in her diary on October 19, 1863: "There has been an unusual degree of housebreaking & stealing going on lately: the latter art being not confined to professional artists but women and even ladies, whom one would not think of suspecting of such meanness have been detected in the act of purloining hats, dress goods, etc., from the stores. One lady was detected by a shopkeeper in carrying off several pieces of dress goods, and the merchant knowing who she was followed her home, accused her of it before her father and made them pay him the value of the goods." In December she wrote, "People have been detected going out from town with wagons, to the country, and stealing loads of wood, fowls, corn, etc., from the farmers, which they afterward bring to town and sell, either to groceries, or at the camps."[20]

The Union army had changed its strategy since earlier abandoning Lexington. Now the Federals constructed forts for the protection of the city. One of these, Fort Clay, went up not far from the Brezing grocery, off the turnpike to Versailles. This quadrangle earthwork, surrounded by a ditch, was accessed by way of a drawbridge. Along its exterior walls the fort "bristled with sharp pointed stakes ready for the impalement of raiding rebels," Rev. Pratt wrote.[21] The Union troops constructed another earthen fort near the top of the homestretch of the Kentucky Association racecourse on the city's east end.

A racetrack might have seemed a peculiar place to build a fort, especially this racetrack, one of the few places where the sport actually managed to continue through the war. The track did come perilously close to closing on June 4, 1861, because of military skirmishes. The association had held only two races over two days, one each day, indicating a shortage of horses. At the end of the second day the track closed its gates. A note in the official racing records reads: "This meeting seems to have been abandoned by reason of the war; Lexington, being the scene on several occasions of active hostilities."[22]

Indeed, the war would alter the practices of Bluegrass horsemen. New racetracks opened during the war at Saratoga Springs, New York, and Paterson, New Jersey, offering much richer purses than the track at Lexington could. Kentuckians took advantage of these new opportunities and shipped their horses north. Racing continued in Lexington, but on a limited basis. The Kentucky Association track operated throughout the rest of the war, but it was not what it had been.

You took your chances if you chose to keep your horses in Kentucky during the war, especially toward the end when horses had become scarce. A number of horse owners in Lexington and the nearby countryside sold off their stock at vastly reduced prices, which they must have thought was better than seeing them stolen or impressed by the army, Confederate or Union. Peter wrote in her diary: "A gentleman from Clark County was in town with a fine lot of horses which he sold for little or nothing, one splendid horse going for $90 as he said he would rather take what he could get for them than let the rebels have them."[23] Toward war's end, outlaws began stealing from the stock farms. They particularly favored Robert Alexander's estate, Woodburn, and those of his neighbors in Woodford County, west of Lexington.

In June 1864 Morgan raided Lexington once more. But by this time, Morgan had lost control of his men. Lacking leadership and discipline, the raiders wreaked havoc. They set off at a full gallop for the Kentucky Association track, where they thought they might find racehorses in training belonging to an outspoken Unionist, James. A. Grinstead. Morgan's men discovered Grinstead's pair of barns empty of horses, but they burned the stables nevertheless. The raiders also burned a large government horse and mule corral on Third Street. They set fire to a brewery. Rev. Pratt wrote that the Union soldiers retreated to Fort Clay and from there shelled the city fiercely, trying to turn back the Confederate raiders. "It was frightful to see those missiles of death whizzing over our heads." While citizens hid inside their homes, Morgan's men looted downtown clothing and hat stores and the shop of a saddler. They also robbed the Lexington branch of the Bank of Kentucky. They forced people to give up their watches, money, and guns. They raided a livery stable for horses and then rode out the Richmond Road to the Clay estate, Ashland, where they stole $25,000 worth of Thoroughbreds.[24]

In April 1865, Lexington received word of Confederate general Robert E. Lee's surrender at Appomattox Court House in Virginia. After four long years, the war everyone had thought would be over in a mere thirty days had finally come to an end. Unionists in Lexington poured out of their homes and shops, cheering and celebrating as they filled the streets. Bells tolled. Guns fired in celebration from Fort Clay on Versailles Road.

Young Belle was nearly five years old. The Lexington that would shape her as she grew up was a city deeply affected by war and a new

racial order. The conflict left Lexington a legacy of smoldering resent-
ments, leading to more violence and lawlessness. At the same time,
Belle's own small world was wrought with violence as she watched
Brezing beat her mother in fits of rage.

chapter **THREE**

A Troubled Youth

On a day in the early fall of 1866, Belle walked across Main Street to an entirely different world. She was six years old and heading for her first day of school. As a younger child, Belle would have watched her sister, Hester, cross this street to attend No. 2 Harrison School. Now Hester was off in a new direction, enrolled at Dudley School on Maxwell Street.[1]

A neighbor, Linda Neville, said the girls were always well clothed because their mother sewed charming outfits for them. Despite her nice clothes, Belle soon realized that her new classmates would have nothing to do with her. The children at school avoided Belle just as neighbors shunned the Brezing family. A classmate revealed to Belle that her mother had threatened to whip her if she played with "the Brezing girl."[2]

George and Sarah's drunken rages were scandalous enough, but Belle's mother had heightened the family's notoriety by suing her husband for divorce. Belle began school three months after the divorce, and the talk had not yet died down. No wonder her classmates avoided her. In the months following the lawsuit, filed in 1866, titillating revelations about the Brezings emerged, fueling the small city's big appetite for gossip.

The problem was not so much that Brezing drank, if you believed the talk. It turned out that Sarah was quite the harlot. Brezing, fighting as fiercely in court as he had at the grocery, dragged his saloon pals into the fray to swear that Sarah had driven her husband to drink. James R. Heatherington told the court he witnessed Sarah and a female companion drinking one evening in the back room of a saloon. Nothing surprising about that, given Sarah's habits, but according to Heatherington, Sarah and the saloon's proprietor then slipped off to an upstairs room— where the only furniture was a mattress. The two returned a short while later, but before long Sarah and another man went together into a front room, closing the door behind them. She came back soon afterward to continue drinking. At the end of the night, Sarah took the saloonkeeper home with her. Heatherington also testified that he had seen Sarah at a house of prostitution: "I am satisfied that her conduct has been such as to indicate her to be a woman of ill fame, and unchaste."[3] Heatherington did not explain what he himself was doing at the brothel, but his report that Sarah had been there was bad news for a woman in a divorce case.

Brezing's drinking pals collaborated closely in their relation of one particular incident that took place at a local drinking emporium known as Cook's Saloon. John Worth said he recalled seeing Sarah and a female companion come into the saloon, where "she drank one glass after another until she drank about 7 or 8 glasses and scattered the bear [*sic*] all over the room." Later, Sarah threw an apple at her husband who, his friends said, had been sitting in the saloon minding his own business. Sarah's aim was true. The apple hit Brezing square in the nose, bringing blood. Worth said the drinking continued after the apple hit its mark, "until they got very drunk."[4]

Worth had not overlooked the possibility of having his own good time on the night of the bloody apple. After Sarah and her companion went home, he too departed the saloon for the Brezing house, although he was more interested in Sarah's friend. How much weirdness could you count in a night at the Brezing house? A lot, as it turned out. At some point, Sarah came into the room where Worth and the woman were entertaining themselves. There, she dressed in men's clothing and informed them she was going out again.[5]

Sarah obtained her divorce from George, although the records fail to mention whether she received the alimony she sought. Sarah's life moved at a fast pace; before long she had married another man, William McMeekin. He was slightly younger than Sarah and employed as a carriage painter. Sarah and the girls moved in with McMeekin, and Sarah changed her own surname and the girls' to his. However, this arrangement did not last long. By 1875 Sarah, also known as "Sallie," listed herself in directories as a widow, although it appears that she was merely separated from her husband, who lived nearby.[6]

In 1871, Hester moved out of Sarah's household. Hester had received a marriage proposal from a commercial painter named John "Pick" Norton, surely welcome in its promise of transporting Hester out of her mother's unstable life. Belle, now eleven, would not see much of Hester after the marriage. Perhaps Belle did grow up as a sad and lonely girl, as her biographer, E. I. "Buddy" Thompson, speculated. Little is known of her childhood, although she certainly worked hard at school, occasionally earning certificates called awards of merit.[7]

Sarah continued to make the family's home in the west end of Lexington, a neighborhood that had declined significantly since the antebellum era. During the 1830s, Robert Todd, a respected grocer and politician, had lived in a two-story brick house on West Main Street. One of his daughters, Mary Todd, eventually married Abraham Lincoln. But by now the neighborhood had turned into an assortment of dwellings mixed in with physicians' offices, hide tanneries, dry goods shops, and saloons, plus a coal dealer, a hemp factory, a feed mill, and a carriage maker. Distilleries, slaughterhouses, and woolen mills also occupied these streets. "The structures along Main from Merino to Cemetery gate and along the railroad & Town Branch were mostly of a cheap class," recalled a physician, Joseph M. Tanner, in his memories of old Lexington. The neighborhood had slipped badly.[8]

The west end was not alone in this decline. Numerous parts of Lexington presented a grim picture, quite in contrast to the bucolic Eden and civilized city that Bluegrass boosters promoted in describing horse country. All you heard about were the picturesque estates of landowners, and indeed grand estates clearly dotted the countryside, and pockets of substantial urban dwellings spoke to the prosperous circumstances of their owners. But the immense wealth of Lexington and the surrounding area was juxtaposed with extreme poverty. Much went untold about the many textures of Bluegrass lifestyle, from rural hamlets where black farm workers dwelt to the city center where poverty, crime, and social disorder rendered portions of Lexington filthy and dangerous.

Part of the problem was machine politics ruled by city bosses. Machine politics were endemic in American cities from the end of the Civil War through the Gilded Age; in some cities, the machines carried on into the middle of the twentieth century. Bosses doled out every form of patronage from Christmas turkeys to jobs for the loyal city dwellers whose votes the bosses controlled. Bosses ran their districts and even entire cities like benevolent dictators, filling their pockets with bribes and payoffs from those who wished to conduct business within the boss's ward. In New York, William M. Tweed's gang ruled. His acolyte, George Washington Plunkett, was so successful that he wrote the definitive book about how to succeed at boss politics. In Philadelphia, Boise Penrose and the notorious Republican machine held sway. In Lexington, Dennis Mulligan ran the city like his own kingdom, benevolent to his friends and those who lined his pockets.

Thoroughly infused with the boss tradition, Mulligan believed, as historian Duane Bolin has written, that informal government like his patronage system was the only type of government truly representative of the people. According to Bolin, "Mulligan viewed politics not as a way of bringing progress to the city of Lexington but as a means of bettering his own lot. It was his business." Mulligan safeguarded his "business" by seeing that no other factions invaded his turf. Consequently, Lexington remained mired in the past and short on modern urban improvement. Reformers did not begin to break Mulligan's stranglehold on city hall until the 1880s. Before then, he successfully staved off all attempts to bring modernity to Lexington, whether for maintenance of poorly kept streets or the building of a water-treatment plant. He opposed bringing manufacturing to Lexington, saying it was unnecessary. He tried to hold off the arrival of the telephone. The kindest way to describe his management style is "old school."[9]

In 1879, Mulligan detoured temporarily from his obstructionist habits to permit construction of a new municipal market house not far from the dwelling Belle occupied with her mother. Mulligan had good reason for changing tactics. He quickly discerned that the location of the new market house would enhance the value of his own property. He approved construction with a caveat: the new building had to be set back ten feet from the street so people could see his grocery sitting prominently on the corner. Lexington was Mulligan's alone to portion out to his pals, and like Plunkett in New York and Penrose in Philadelphia, he suffered no opposition.[10]

Among the municipal failings in Lexington, access to clean drinking water ranked as most serious. When Belle was a girl in the 1870s, most people in Lexington drew their water from wells, springs, and cisterns. The enlightened portion of the citizenry that pleaded with Mulligan's government for a filtration treatment plant met with persistent, stubborn opposition. Water also flowed through the center of the city along a section of the Elkhorn Creek that people had long called the Town Fork, or Town Branch. This water carried all sorts of refuse, including the by-products of the distilleries along the creek. Citizens continued to pressure Mulligan for a treatment plant for filtering their water. But they would have to wait until the 1880s, after Mulligan's faction no longer held the city in its powerful grip.

City authorities had fought a long-running battle with the distilleries over dumping garbage into the Town Branch. Grand juries in Fayette County had been indicting distilleries since at least 1870, but the distilleries appeared to see their fines as nothing more than a cost of doing business. As late as 1885, after Lexington finally got a water-treatment plant, the Commonwealth of Kentucky indicted the James Pepper distillery for dumping "slops and offal" from the distillery into the Town Branch Creek.[11]

People also drank directly from the numerous limestone springs that bubbled up through the soil all over the Bluegrass, even in downtown streets. Joseph Tanner could recall seeing a spring emerging from a cave in the cellar of a business on Main Street between Upper and Mill streets. He had heard that water also flowed beneath a building at the northwest corner of Water and Upper streets.[12] Public springs in various parts of the city usually were outfitted with hand pumps that anyone could operate by manually lifting and lowering a large wooden handle. One such pump pulled water up from the spring bubbling close to the surface on the southwest corner of the Court House lot. The spring reportedly supplied abundant water. These springs had served their purpose during Lexington's early days, but as the city grew, people began to connect the dots between their drinking water and disease— or at least with an unpleasant smell or taste. More visionary citizens began to fear that surface filth was contaminating spring water. Those who could afford to build cisterns did so, catching rainwater falling off their roofs.

Americans of the 1870s did not understand germ theory as they would twenty years later, but some things had begun to make sense: privies in Lexington backyards all too often existed in proximity to drinking wells. Could one be seeping into the other, especially after heavy spring rains?

Water concerns did not end with drinking supplies. Fire was a constant danger to nineteenth-century buildings, and no city could fight fire effectively without ready access to water. Throughout the city center, public cisterns served as reservoirs for fire fighting. These large cylindrical or rectangular cisterns were built alongside the streets.[13] The problem with these cisterns was that they did not always contain much water. Lexington went through cyclical dry spells, and these dry spells proved especially challenging for fire fighters when water levels in the cisterns fell too low. When Belle was eleven years old, in 1871, two fires during August caused major damage.

The first fire began at the corner of Main and Upper streets, at Barnes' and Woods' drugstore. The city's two steam engines, which horses pulled to the scene, failed to operate at capacity because of defective hoses and a lack of water in the cisterns. The second fire broke out at Main Street at Broadway and quickly spread to a nearby residential neighborhood. This second fire destroyed more than half of the block between Main and Short streets, but it could have been worse. Residents checked the fire's progress by passing buckets filled with water. After these two devastating fires, work began on construction of additional cisterns. Someone came up with a plan to connect all the cisterns, but the city council did not take to the idea. Perhaps Mulligan's government thought that concept too progressive for Lexington's needs.[14]

The Lexington of Belle's youth was not large. Boundaries extended one mile in each direction from the city center. Beyond these boundaries lay the countryside. People traveled to Lexington by stagecoach or railroad, on horseback or in wagons and buggies. Those employing the latter conveyances had to endure the bump and grind of streets paved with rocks the size of a man's fist.[15]

Italian, German, and Irish immigrants lived among the Kentucky-born locals, many of whom were descended from pioneers who had crossed through the Cumberland Gap from Virginia and North Carolina or floated down the Ohio River from Pittsburgh on flatboats. Among the newcomers, Dionesio Mucci and his brother, Zachariah, emigrated from Italy, living briefly in Ohio before settling in Kentucky. They moved to Lexington in 1864. Three years later, the brothers purchased a house facing West Main at Georgetown Street and an adjoining lot that connected in back to the residence and faced Georgetown. Dionesio Mucci was to figure prominently in young Belle's life.[16]

Dionesio Mucci occupied the house with his wife, Frederich, his brother, Zachariah, and his wife, Angeline, and Zachariah and Angeline's two sons, Emile and Henry. The house stood not far from where Belle lived and attended school. Behind the Mucci house, facing Georgetown Street, stood the hide, iron, and paper business that Dionesio opened under the name Mucci & Bro. Dionesio drove a wagon pulled by a blind bay horse and went about Lexington buying scrap metal, rags, and paper. Zachariah may have assisted his brother at the tannery and scrap yard business, but he listed his main occupation in the city directory as "musician."[17]

Before long, Dionesio, in his thirties, had befriended young Belle. Not long afterward, in 1872, Dionesio and twelve-year-old Belle began a sexual relationship. This was not a passing fancy for either of them. The two remained in a relationship for at least two years and maybe longer.[18]

Kentuckians of the time entertained an array of ideas concerning girls of Belle's age. At one end of this spectrum stood the age of consent in Kentucky: twelve. At the other end stood a class-based belief that young girls should remain chaste for many years beyond their twelfth birthday, until they were married to a respectable young man. A notable proponent of the latter view, William Campbell Preston Breckinridge, addressed the young of Kentucky on occasion about the merits of remaining chaste. Breckinridge was a man of considerable standing. During the Civil War, he had attained the rank of colonel in the Confederate cavalry. He was a lawyer, politician, and journalist. Kentuckians elected him to Congress, where he served from 1885 to 1895.

During the same year that young Belle and Mucci began a sexual relationship, Breckinridge addressed students at the Bourbon County

Female College, urging them to remain chaste. In another talk, at Sayre School in Lexington, Breckinridge counseled the female students to shun the popular practice among young ladies of rubbing their cheeks with flannel rags to produce a beguiling blush. Breckinridge also pleaded with the girls to avoid rumpled hair, believing this might draw the sexual notice of young men. He advised the girls to avoid "useless hand-shaking, promiscuous kissing, needless touches."[19]

This sounded like wholesome advice from an inspirational role model. So people in Lexington later were shocked to learn that Breckinridge had kept a mistress throughout his tenure in Washington. Her name was Madeline Valeria Pollard. This hot gossip item became public knowledge after the death of Breckinridge's wife, Issa Desha, and the congressman's subsequent marriage to his cousin Louise Wing. Pollard, who had believed all along that she would become the next Mrs. Breckinridge, now found herself a woman scorned. She sued the congressman for breach of promise.[20]

Belle thus became a "ruined" woman at an early age in a community holding highly conflicted ideas about young girls. Breckinridge's ideals had little relevance in the world in which Belle lived. Belle and Mucci continued their relationship. In 1874, he gave her a scrapbook inscribed, "To Miss Belle Brezing Lexington, Ky. Presented by Mr. D. Mucci Feb. 14, 1874."[21] Belle was fourteen years old. She must have prized her scrapbook, for she filled it with colorful clippings from magazines as well as with Valentine cards, photographs, and a poem she composed titled "Kisses." The poem reveals much about young Belle's longing for love:

> Sitting to night in my chamber,
> a school girl figure and lonely,
> I kiss the end of my finger.
> that and that only.
> Reveries rises from the smokey mouth
> Memories linger surround me.
> Boys that are married or single.
> Gather round me. School boys in pantalets romping,
> Boys that now are growing to be young lads,
> Boys that like to be kissed, and like to give kisses.

Kisses—well I remember them;
Those in the corner were fleetest;
Sweet were those on the sly in the Dark were the sweetest
Girls are tender and gentle,
To woo was almost to win them.
They lips are good as ripe peaches, and cream for finger.
Girls are sometimes flirts, and coquettish;
Now catch and kiss if you can sin;
Could I catch both—ah, wasn't I a happy Girl,
Boys is pretty and blooming sweetly, yea
Sweetness over their rest
Them I loved dearly and truly, Last and the best.
           —Written by Belle Brezing, Lexington, Ky.[22]

The poem implies that Belle had many suitors in addition to Mucci. She also had acquired three close friends her own age: Kate Parker, Sallie P. Martin, and Willie Sutphin. Sallie revealed a schoolgirl crush when she wrote in Belle's scrapbook,

Belle
I'll give my heart to you
If you'll give yours to me
We'll lock them up together
And throw away the key.
           —Sallie

Another greeting from Sallie was titled "Love to Belle":

I love my love in the morning
For Belle's fair and sweetly fair
Her blushing cheeks in crimson streak
Its clouds Belle golden fair
           Your trusting friend
           Sallie P. Martin

A third greeting from Sallie read,

To Belle
Friendship may weave a garland
Gold may link a chain;
But love alone can form a clasp
Forever to remain.

From your most sincere
Schoolmate, Sallie [23]

The scrapbook reveals much about Belle and the loneliness she experienced as a young girl. One handwritten inscription begins, "No one to lose, none to caress, roaming alone through this world's wilderness, dead is my heart, joy is unknown, for in my sorrow I am weeping alone."[24] The writing does not appear to be Belle's when compared with her handwriting in the poem "Kisses." But the words must have resonated with her for her to include them in her scrapbook.

Willie also copied a poem in Belle's scrapbook, revealing that he shared Belle's feelings of loneliness:

A Gentleman's Wish
I've often wished to have a friend,
With whom my choice hours to spend,
To whom I safely might impart
Each dream and weakness of my heart,
And who would every sorrow hear,
And mingle with my grief a tear,
And to secure that bliss for life,
I'd wish for that friend to be my wife.

Yours truly,
Willie Sutphin.[25]

A few months after writing this poem, Willie Sutphin would be dead. He and a young friend, George Sharp, were playing with a small pistol on Mill Street near Dudley School. The gun fired accidentally, and Sharp shot Willie just below the left eye. He died two days later. With this incident, Belle had lost one of the few people with whom she is known to have formed a friendship. She was growing up much too quickly in a world that had never spared her feelings.[26]

Mucci remained in Belle's life, even after she took up with a young man closer to her age, Johnny Cook. Johnny was a year older than Belle. His father, Philip Koch, a German, had run a saloon on Mulberry Street (later renamed Limestone Street) before he died. Johnny's stepfather, a German named Frederick Gobel (sometimes spelled Goebel), ran a saloon on Broadway between Main and Short streets. Soon after Belle's fifteenth birthday in 1875, Johnny Cook would meet a tragic end in a love triangle with Belle at the center.[27]

It happened this way: at fifteen, Belle became pregnant. Three months into her pregnancy, she surprised everyone by marrying James Kenney, nineteen, an apprentice at the trade of cigar making. He appeared almost out of nowhere in Belle's life. By this time, Belle had developed such widespread notoriety that people far beyond the west end of Lexington knew her name. This celebrity status was quite remarkable for a girl of fifteen, and we can only wonder how it had come about. But at any rate, the *Lexington Daily Press* found her such a hot gossip personality that it reported on the marriage: the teenage harlot had taken a husband and would be a single woman no more. The newspaper's story made fun of Belle and her marriage ceremony, just as everyone in her neighborhood had been making fun of her for years: "A marriage in high life is reported between Miss Belle Brezing and Mr. James Kinney [*sic*]. The ceremony was performed at the residence of the bride's mother. It was brief but most significant, performed in a manner so touching that it drew tears from the eyes of those who witnessed it. La Belle Brezing is no more. She is now Mistress Kinney."[28]

Belle's marriage appears to have been a liaison of convenience, for apparently she had no intention of ending her relationship with either Johnny Cook or Mucci. Belle's biographer, Thompson, suggested that Belle and/or her mother might have persuaded Kenney to marry the girl, or even tricked Kenney into the marriage, in order to give Belle's child a father. If Belle and Kenney ever lived together as a married couple it was at Sarah's house, for Belle continued to reside with her mother.

But the other men did not leave Belle's life.

Nine days after the wedding, Belle wrote a note to Johnny Cook:

Dear One:—Here it is and I want you to write to me when you go and believe me your truly girl as every, send me yours and don't forget it either.

> Your darling
> Belle

Belle wrote Cook a second note which, like the first, was found in his pocket after his body was discovered in an alley behind Jefferson Street between Main and Short streets:

Dearest One:—I will be down town at three o'clock look out for me. I will go to the office and by the store. Ma has come, have my pistol for me.[29]

Johnny Cook was found dead in the alley with a bullet wound to his head. A derringer lay either by his side or on his chest, according to which account you believed. The big question was whether he had shot himself or someone had murdered him. The crowd that gathered to stare at Cook's body debated these possibilities in earnest. The *Lexington Daily Press* discussed the same question at length. Perhaps the reason for this interest was the specter of Belle at the center of the mystery. And as everyone in Lexington knew, Belle Brezing always made for the most fascinating stories. The headline in the *Lexington Daily Press* read: "A SUICIDE OR A MURDER: A Young Man Is Found Dead, with a Pistol by His Side, in an Alley on Georgetown Street."[30]

At the scene of Cook's death, the crowd prevailed upon a lawyer passing by to accept the hasty appointment of coroner so that light could be shed right then and there on the circumstances of this young man's death. The lawyer convened an inquest at the crime scene. He searched Cook's pockets and found 60¢ in cash, some cigars, and the notes from Belle. He also found a lock of hair and a photograph of a young woman, presumably Belle. On the back of the photograph someone had written in pencil: "Put this close to my heart."[31]

With this brief inquest hurriedly completed, the crowd loaded Cook's body onto a wagon to return him to his family's home. His mother and father had arrived at the crime scene late, and the mother collapsed with hysteria. The tension was building rapidly. Where Belle was at the time is unknown. As the wagon departed for the Cook residence, more commotion ensued. The city's officially appointed coroner, John Byrne, intercepted the wagon and immediately dismissed the findings of the impromptu coroner. The official coroner insisted that he would hold a proper inquest to be convened later at the municipal offices. This man had no intention of retreating from a case that was rapidly assuming a high profile, for Belle's name was now whispered on the wind.[32]

Those who knew Cook or had seen him earlier that day expressed bafflement at his death. Cook had seemed in good humor, so it did not make sense that he would have killed himself. But the case soon took an interesting twist: the newspaper learned that Cook worked in the same cigar shop as Belle's new husband and that the photograph in Cook's pocket was in truth of Belle. The newspaper also discovered that Cook indeed had met with Belle, as her notes had requested, and that witnesses had seen him walking her home to her mother's place, where she lived with her new husband. After parting with Belle, Cook went into a saloon on Main Street, where he bought some cigars and talked about relocating to Cincinnati. "It is useless to disguise a fact that is well known," the newspaper reporter wrote, "that the young woman referred to in this sad affair, is Miss Belle Brezing, who married a few days ago a young man named Kinney, working in the same shop with Cook; that it was her picture the deceased had received that day; that he had met her as the notes intimated, and that he was seen walking home with her." Now everyone's interest stood riveted on Cook's death. The news became the hottest gossip in town.[33]

As gossip spread, so did a new speculation: perhaps someone had murdered Cook. But who? The newspaper called the shooting "one of the most unfortunate tragedies that have ever shocked the people of this community."[34] This was an exaggeration, of course. But the young man's death did not lack for high drama because of the cast of characters involved. And what of Belle? Did she grieve for young Johnny Cook, who had held her photo close to his heart until his death? Did she consider that he might have taken his own life out of despair over losing her to this newcomer on the scene, James Kenney? Or had Kenney, Cook's workmate, shot the young man? It is unknown if Mucci came under suspicion, but he possibly should have. Johnny Cook's death remained a hot topic.

As the story unfolded over several days, Lexington residents remained eager for some glimpse inside the wayward Belle's inner soul. Soon they received a spectacular insight in the form of a poem published in the *Lexington Leader* under Belle's name:

Johnnie Cook—Gone to his Rest
His busy hands are folded,
His work on earth is done;
His trials all are ended,
His heavenly crown is won.

Upon his brow so peaceful
No earthly shadows rest;
For anxious cares reach never
The mansions of the blest

Within the home he brightened
His quiet course has run—A life of pure unselfishness—
   A man's work well done.

No titles high and sounding,
Shed such a holy light
As crowns that brow so faded,
Now passed from earthly blight.

The sad and lonely household
Will miss his guiding hand;
The daughters, loving, clinging,
Without his aid must stand.

The children, mother's counsel
Will seek, on earth, no more;
No more his hand will lead them,
Save on the heavenly shore.

The flowers he loved and tended
Are nipped by wintry frost;
His life with theirs departed,
O'ershadowed, but not lost.

For in the Spring time coming
They'll burst the prison bond;
So, too, that form, now lifeless,
Will rise to life beyond.

There on the shores eternal
His spirit beckoning stands,
Still guiding on his loved ones
To join the heavenly bands.
Sept. 24th, 1875.

Most likely, some newsroom hack had cranked out this literary effort in a twisted burst of creativity. Belle surely was not the poet, for the piece rhymes too well, unlike the earlier, unsophisticated effort at poetry found in her scrapbook. Moreover, an odd note to the editor accompanied this poem, which makes the poem's source even more doubtful. The note read: "Please put this in the Press and Dispatch if want pay, send me word Oblige Belle Brezing."[35] The men of the newsroom surely enjoyed a great guffaw.

The excitement was not over. Kenney, new husband of "La Belle Brezing," went on the lam, disappearing either before or just after the shooting. What did this say about his role in Johnny Cook's death or his place in Belle's true feelings? We can only speculate. But he did not immediately return to Lexington—not for a long time, and long after Belle surely had moved on with her life.

Meanwhile, the second (and official) coroner's inquest convened within its proper setting in the municipal offices. The outcome was the same, however: the coroner ruled that Cook had killed himself. This ruling failed to stem the gossip that perhaps someone had murdered Cook. And people were not about to let it go. New reports surfaced: someone had seen a man on the Brezings' property moments after the shooting. Belle swore that the back gate to her mother's place had been nailed shut. However, as the newspaper reported, people found the gate open after Cook's death. The person who found the body saw the pistol lying some distance from Cook. Moments later, someone saw the pistol lying on the deceased's chest. How could the gun have moved by itself? Why would someone have moved the gun? The lack of police investigation was remarkable. The newspaper asked: "Why was not Belle Brezing forced to tell who was in the house at the time of the killing? Why did young Koch [Johnny Cook] come away from Belle Brezing's house without giving up the pistol as he had intended, in answer to the request contained in Belle Brezing's note?"[36] And, you have to wonder, why did Belle Brezing want a pistol?

Then Mucci entered the picture. It turned out he was the last person to see Cook alive, not two minutes before the young man's death. The newspaper then hung out a gossipy teaser for all to ponder: "A gentleman in this city, whose name will not be mentioned unless the case comes before the grand jury, believes, from a remark which he overheard a night or two before, that it was not a suicide; but he will not state what he heard." This newspaper story reflected what many, no doubt, already had wondered. The newspaper was speculating that Johnny Cook had met with foul play "and the public sentiment will not be satisfied until there is a more thorough and searching investigation."[37]

Thompson, Belle's biographer, identified James Kenney as the prime suspect in Cook's death. In fact, if a love triangle had enveloped Belle, Cook, and Kenney, this conclusion would make sense. Kenney did not return to Lexington until 1887, after an absence of more than ten years. When he did come back, he did not stay long. Thompson wrote, "If he ever saw his wife Belle again, it was only in passing on the street."[38]

On March 14, 1876, Belle gave birth to a girl and named her Daisy May Kenney. The identity of the father remained as much a mystery as how her friend Johnny Cook had died and what role Belle had played in this affair.

chapter FOUR

A Businesswoman
Whose Business Was Men

B elle's life was spinning out of control. Johnny Cook was dead, she had just given birth to Daisy May, and now Sarah, her mother, was seriously ill. The nature of Sarah's malady is unknown. Many illnesses plagued Americans in the 1870s—typhoid, cholera, tuberculosis, small-pox, and syphilis, to name a few—and medical knowledge about com-municable diseases was limited.[1] If you were lucky when you became ill, you recovered. But you could not always trust your luck. Sarah's was running out.

It is not known where Sarah spent her final days. Belle may have cared for her at home. Lexington's first public hospital did not open until the following year, 1877, when five Catholic Sisters of Charity established the St. Joseph Hospital in a house near the corner of Lin-den Walk and Maxwell Street.[2] But if Sarah suffered from a conta-gious disease, such as smallpox, she likely would have spent her last days in a shelter commonly known as the "pest house." It was so named not because people understood germ theory, which they did not, but because the city viewed the stricken as "pests" to be locked up, seques-tered from society—and out of its view. The term "pest house" held pow-erful class connotations. The upper classes, no matter how ill, would never be categorized as "pests."[3]

A disease like smallpox always put city residents on high alert.[4] One example in Lexington occurred in January 1881, five years after Sarah's illness, when a handful of people stricken with smallpox turned up in

Lexington. City authorities hit the panic button. They soon learned the mayor of Cincinnati had dispatched these unfortunates from Cincinnati's pest house on a train bound for Lexington. Certainly this was one way to dispose of the unwanted. Taking his cue from Cincinnati, Lexington mayor C. M. Johnson had them put on a train bound for Somerset, south of Lexington. No one thought to consult the smallpox victims about their wishes, however; they slipped from the marshal's clutches before the train departed Lexington, undoubtedly leaving authorities red faced with confusion and embarrassment. Two days later, a sharp-eyed citizen noticed them in a rented house along a stretch off South Mulberry Street (later South Limestone Street) named Branch Alley. This alley, running along the rear of the Phoenix Hotel between Mulberry and Rose streets, received its name from the Town Branch Creek that ran parallel to the back of the hotel. Denizens of Branch Alley led lives as polluted as the creek, and contemporaries knew the alley as "a hotbed of sin and wretchedness and abode of filth and misery."[5] No surprise that the smallpox victims had chosen to hide out there; few on Branch Alley would have cared to come into contact with the authorities. But city officials were on a mission to catch these people, and they did. Once they got them, however, the authorities had no idea what to do with them. Lexington no longer had a pest house; it had burned to the ground.

Before the smallpox could spread, as everyone feared it would, city officials needed to act quickly. They quarantined the rented house. They also hung out a yellow flag to warn people there was smallpox within. They debated establishing a new pest house, a rental property on the Winchester Pike that someone offered to the city for a $500 annual fee. But they had overlooked the inevitable outcry this would raise in the surrounding neighborhood and were forced to consider an alternate plan. Eventually, officials decided to open a pest house on Sixth Street alongside a field where the indigent were buried. No one lived within two hundred yards of this place, so officials expected no complaints. They moved the stricken people to the potter's field shack in a wagon. Meanwhile, someone in city chambers came up with the proactive idea of vaccinating everyone in the city who hadn't yet been vaccinated against smallpox. But was it too late? Was the disease already on the march?

The smallpox crisis did not end with moving the victims to Sixth Street. Soon a city councilman discovered that some attendants at the pest house were slipping into the city at night to amuse themselves. Just when the authorities thought they had contained the disease, the very people charged with keeping the quarantine were busting loose for a good time. Alarm spread quickly. The mayor responded with a warning to the pest house guards: they would be prosecuted if seen again in Lexington.

How serious the crisis was is open to speculation, although by the first of March, city physician Richard Taylor reported that he had treated eighteen smallpox cases during February. This would indicate the disease had indeed spread, although not in epidemic proportions. Four among the stricken had died (the city sold one victim's watch, apparently in an effort to recoup some of the expenses it had incurred), nine remained at the pest house, and others had departed with a clean bill of health. "The sanitary condition of the city is tolerably good," Dr. Taylor concluded after two months of working to contain a breakout of this much-feared disease. He had done the best he could.[6]

Whether it was smallpox or no, Belle must have felt helpless through Sarah's illness. She was a teenager with a new baby and a dying mother. And then Sarah was gone. On May 19, 1876, two months after the birth of Belle's daughter, Sarah passed away. Belle believed her to be forty years old.[7] Belle, just fifteen and unexpectedly on her own, faced grim prospects for the future. Sarah, who had listed her occupation as a dressmaker, might have instructed Belle in sewing techniques. But Belle either could not or chose not to pursue this honest profession.

The *Lexington Daily Press* did not acknowledge the death of Sarah McMeekin. Lexington residents had much more to think about than one woman with a tarnished reputation. Most people were still shaken from a fire the morning of May 15, five days before Sarah's death. The conflagration had destroyed seventeen buildings, but the most serious loss was that of the Phoenix Hotel because this directly affected the opening of the race meet at the Kentucky Association track, the most important event in town. The Phoenix Hotel always had been the most popular place for horsemen and gamblers to stay when in Lexington for the races and horse auctions. The spring race meet at the Kentucky Association track was now in progress, and this hotel, where rooms cost $2 a day and meals 50¢, had been filled to capacity when the fire occurred. Betting was conducted within the hotel as well. Tracks did not then handle betting money; most betting took place off track, through the auctioning of wagering "pools" on horses running in the next day's races. Pools were being sold in the hotel when the cry went up that the place was on fire. The confusion that followed saw guests scattering and "quite a conflagration" taking place. The fire reduced attendance at the racetrack the next day because hotel guests had lost both their belongings and a place to stay.[8]

The fire broke out twice: first along Branch Alley and South Mulberry Street about 1:45 a.m. and a second time about 5:00 a.m. Livery stables, houses, and a grocery were among other buildings destroyed. At A. G. Karsner's Stable, the anguished cries of five horses unable to escape "were terrible to hear," people would read in the newspaper. The horses perished. The newspaper reported that a strong wind propelled a cloud of sparks and blazing embers onto a great number of roofs. In the darkness before dawn, the ominous cloud was visible for miles.[9]

As well as details about the fire, Lexington residents turned to their newspapers for word on the Kentucky Derby, run just prior to the opening of the Lexington race meet. Vagrant had won the Derby by half a length. Now that the races had moved on from Louisville to Lexington, Gus Jaubert announced he would hang up the race results daily in his saloon. Another reason to stop in for a drink: he was known widely for concocting a most delectable burgoo.[10]

Sarah McMeekin's burial was held in the wake of the disastrous fire. A wagon would have transported her body to the new Catholic burial ground called Calvary Cemetery, which had opened two years previously on the Leestown turnpike at the city's west end. A decade later, Belle commissioned a large monument to her mother that she had installed on a twelve-grave site she purchased at this cemetery. The monument reads simply:

Sarah McMeekin
Born May 5, 1836
Died May 19, 1876

Belle attended the burial, probably holding her young daughter close. Belle's sister, Hester, attended in the company of her husband, John Norton. The only other person present might have been a neighbor, a

Mrs. Barnett, who attended possibly out of kindness to young Belle. Rain fell intermittently, as it had the two previous days.[11]

The ground was muddy and the going difficult as Belle and Mrs. Barnett made their way back up the slope leading home. They walked beneath the railroad trestle that crossed the point where the Leestown turnpike turned into West Main Street. The hill was so steep that a horse would have struggled.[12] Carrying a baby up the hill would have been a chore on a sunny day. On a rainy day like this, Belle must have felt doubly forlorn.

When they reached Sarah's rented house, Belle was shocked at the sight before them. There on the street, thrown in a pile, lay her belongings and those of her mother. While Belle had attended Sarah's burial, the landlord had cleared out their house. Now their belongings lay on the rain-soaked ground, splashed with mud and manure churned up by passing horses' hooves. Whatever the landlord's reasons for evicting Belle, his timing could not have been worse.[13]

Belle had little or no money and a baby to feed. Given her reputation, she also would have realized that no one would take her in. Where could she go? Who would help her pay for Daisy May's care? Belle faced a future on her own that seemed to hold no hope.

A solution lay close at hand. Mrs. Barnett took Daisy May from Belle's arms and promised to keep the baby until Belle could find a place to live.[14] Belle retrieved a few of her belongings from the pile on the street. Among these was the scrapbook Mucci had given her. Then she started off on her own without any idea where she would stay. We do not know if she sought help from Mucci, or received it if she did. Perhaps Mrs. Barnett gave her a few coins, although it appears she did not offer Belle a room at her house. Whatever happened, Belle did not return to Mrs. Barnett's house to pick up Daisy May. Mrs. Margaret Egbert, the first policewoman in Lexington, said teenage Belle lived for some time on South Mill Street between High and Maxwell streets, near the city center. Her boyfriend at the time made a living by counterfeiting money. Belle walked the streets.[15]

Lexington's streets in 1876 were no place for the faint of heart or weak of stomach. The smells from refuse, the dust in dry weather, and the constant danger brought by fast horses flying by discouraged decent people from walking about. Crossing a street involved negotiating mounds of manure, the occasional dead animal, and sizeable rocks. Lexington "paved" its Main Street with these large stones without bothering to pack the spaces between them with sand or gravel. In this respect, Lexington was no different from most cities. A streetcar driver cursed the rough pavement of Third Avenue in New York in 1889, remarking, "This work's terrible hard on a horse, mainly because of these cursed stones . . . the stones wear 'em out in a few years."[16]

People in downtown Lexington crossed streets at their peril. On most streets, the operators of livery stables trained and drilled horses at speed, sometimes resulting in injury to pedestrians—and occasionally death. Joseph Tanner, in his memoir of growing up in Lexington, said he once saw a speeding horse on Short Street collide with a wagon horse, killing the latter when the protruding shafts of the training cart hitched to the speed horse speared the poor wagon horse at the base of its neck. The poor beast's "heart blood spurt[ed] in a stream as the shafts were withdrawn and the poor animal sank down dead," Tanner wrote. Such sights were common.[17]

Sidewalks of loose and uneven brick were laid along less than half the length of Main Street, which was rough and pocked with holes. When pedestrians walked along the sidewalks, dirty water squirted up onto their clothing. Women's long skirts would soon be filthy. The city had made no improvements beyond a half mile from the courthouse. On hot summer days, piles of horse manure in the streets created quite a stench.[18]

And this was not the worst of it. Hog pens stood in the central part of the city into the 1870s. Cows roamed the streets at night, despite a city ordinance that forbade it. The cows "go into yards and alleys, and into the gardens of citizens," urban residents complained. Garbage and dead dogs were often dumped in the gutters along streets. "The summer months were redolent with undesirable odors," wrote J. W. Pryor, a physician who moved to Lexington from Missouri in 1880. Construction of a sewage system for the good of everyone's health should have ranked as a top city priority, but that wouldn't happen for years. Money and obstructionist politics stood in the way. Meanwhile, the streets just simply stank.[19]

As late as 1890, the year Riley won the Kentucky Derby, the *Lexington Leader* continued to satirize and criticize the unfortunate condition of city streets. The newspaper editorialized in the lines of a loosely constructed poem that resonated with readers:

Portable bridges will soon be in use across Main Street
Even the brick pavement on East Short Street is in the—mud . . .
Fog horns will be heard in the still watches of the night now that
　Main
Street is open for navigation
If persons are reported missing these balmy days the *Leader*
　suggests
that the Main Street canal be dragged for the remains
Wanted—a diver at each crossing on Main Street to rescue
pedestrians who go down in attempting to strike the submerged
crossings.[20]

A Frankfort resident, H. T. Stanton, wrote under the sway of regional prejudice when from the state capital in 1890 he described Lexington for the *Cincinnati Post*. Boosters were calling Lexington "the Queen of the Bluegrass," as they had since 1881 when the city's first chamber of commerce coined this moniker. But Stanton depicted the city as sleeping in her own dust "amid the noxious vapors that rise from her gutters."[21]

Tanner, recalling 1870s Lexington, took issue with livestock sales at Cheapside on county court days, identifying this tradition as "one of the disagreeable features of street life during Lexington's middle period." Tanner found nothing pleasant in the "mangled mass of humanity and animality" with "men, horses, cattle, sheep, and pigs—auctioneers crying the bid, men on foot dodging back and forth among the neighing, bawling, bleating, squealing animals, and for several days afterwards a scene offensive to eyes and nostrils." For years, citizens and businessmen fought the city to remove the livestock auctions from Cheapside, but they found themselves up against the formidable opposition of farmers.[22]

The streets were also mean, as Belle would have realized. Pryor, the physician, wrote about a call he made during the 1880s to a saloon on Short Street, near Broadway. His colleague, J. A. Stucky, had sought his help at a drinking dive named Lell's Saloon, where a man lay dying on the floor. The physicians arrived at Lell's to find the man unconscious. His abdomen had been sliced wide open in a fight. "His intestines were protruding and covered with sawdust from the floor," Pryor wrote. From the way the good doctor described the scene, the man just as well could have been lying in the dust of a horse corral. Pryor assisted Stucky in cleaning and stitching the man's abdomen, later writing with clinical detachment laced with practical humor, "An anesthetic was not necessary—he [the fallen victim] was dead drunk." The physicians stitched the man back together on the filthy floor with Pryor concluding, again tongue-in-cheek, "I think we got all the sawdust out." A priest arrived to give the man the last rites of the Catholic Church just as someone prepared to remove the patient to St. Joseph Hospital. For the physicians, this was all in a day's work. Saloon fights were common occurrences. Thanks to the physicians, this barroom brawler lived.[23]

Decent folk had avoided the South Broadway neighborhood for years. Gangs and houses of prostitution infested this street that intersected Main Street at city center. Saloonkeepers along South Broadway could not or would not keep peace and order in their establishments. The better folk in Lexington feared nothing could be done about Broadway because nothing was being done. How could they expect otherwise given the political machine's remarkable record of taking Lexington backward instead of forward? Broadway as well as North Upper Street both existed as a no-man's-land, lacking law and order, not to mention decency. Belle always lived on or near these streets. A city directory for 1877–1878 showed her residing at Jefferson and Short streets.[24] She reemerged on North Upper Street in 1879.

Sometime after this latter move, Belle's name appeared once more in the newspapers. The incident that put Belle back in the spotlight was her attempted suicide. Belle and a female companion tried to kill themselves one rainy and oppressively hot and humid Thursday, July 24, 1879, by swallowing morphine. By Saturday, the news about these attempted suicides had spread beyond Lexington, with the *Canton (Ohio) Daily Repository* identifying the two women as Belle Brezing and Mollie Canton.[25]

The Lexington newspaper never did identify Belle and her friend by name. Apparently it did not need to. In this gossipy small city, everyone would have known the identity of the girls because everyone downtown would have been talking about this incident. Perhaps Belle was not known in Canton, which could explain why the Ohio newspaper in Canton did identify her when picking up the news items from Lexington. On the other hand, perhaps Belle was so well known beyond Lexington, even as a nineteen-year-old, that the *Canton Daily Repository* did not hesitate to name her.

The newspaper story in Lexington opened thus: "Two unfortunate young girls living on Upper Street in this city, weary with a life of shame, attempted suicide Thursday morning about nine o'clock by taking morphine." Belle and her friend seem to have regretted their action almost as soon as they swallowed their doses. "Five minutes later they told what they had done, when physicians were sent for and antidotes applied," read the account.[26]

The *Lexington Daily Press* must have heard about the incident the previous day, just as the newspaper was preparing to publish. It briefly reported, "Ten grains of morphine is not a very comforting potion, if what is said of the way the doctors treated those girls around yesterday be true." Did this mean that physicians had treated the stricken women by giving them additional morphine to help them withdraw from their overdoses? Or did it mean the two women had been taking morphine for some time, perhaps to the point they were addicted?[27]

This suicide attempt was not Belle's first. She had told others frequently that she was unhappy living the life of a prostitute and would "rather die a thousand deaths than live the life she was then pursuing." The newspaper's reporter wrote that the two women were "weary with shame" over the lives they lived. But those were the reporter's words, couched in his moralism. Belle never gave interviews to the press.[28]

Belle's access to morphine did not place her outside the norm in Lexington or anywhere in the United States. Americans had embarked on an extraordinary drug binge beginning in the 1840s and continuing through the 1890s, partaking of everything from opium to heroin to morphine. The federal government did not prohibit importation of these drugs, nor did it attempt to regulate them. In fact, their presence proliferated in patent medicines that were sold at pharmacies, through newspaper ads, and by disreputable "snake oil" salesmen who peddled their wares on street corners and courthouse squares. Physicians also prescribed treatments that included morphine and heroin.[29]

Addicts existed everywhere throughout society, not simply on the streets that Belle trod. Some addicts functioned quite well despite their habits, as many Lexingtonians probably knew. Around the time that Belle took her near-fatal dose of morphine, the *Lexington Daily Press* reprinted an interview with a notorious drug addict, one Dr. Tyler, a physician who practiced in New York. Tyler blamed his addiction on a buggy accident. He said the tumble he took when thrown from a carriage left him in such excruciating pain that his physicians prescribed morphine, addicting him. The fact that the *Lexington Daily Press* reprinted the interview from a newspaper in New York, the *Mercury,* indicated that perhaps Lexingtonians shared with other Americans a curiosity and a concern about the widespread addiction problems of their day.[30]

Dr. Tyler, presently in jail awaiting trial in New York, had acquired the questionable distinction of being "the greatest morphine consumer in the known world." As the doctor related, he had managed to function in his medical practice while under a hazy cloud of addiction. "While in this condition I would diagnose patients, perform surgery, write prescriptions, all in the most thorough manner," he said, "and as long as the drug lasted I was actually a better man than I ever had been before; but slowly and surely the exhilarating influence would fade, a kind of weariness would come over me, then nervousness, despondency, pain, and finally absolute horror."[31]

The *Lexington Daily Press* noted that thousands of people throughout the United States shared Dr. Tyler's "tragic" story, "and this particular form of indulgence is not confined to men." The *Daily Press* revealed that some women of high standing in Lexington would prefer to rid themselves of the drug habit. One can only wonder who among the socialites slipped morphine into their morning coffee or popped something stronger into their afternoon tea. The *Daily Press* noted of Lexington: "Here in this very city are scores of persons well on the way to the condition so fearfully depicted by this unfortunate, and whose friends are at a loss to know what to do with them."[32]

With this episode of drugs and attempted suicide, Belle appeared to be spiraling down a hole from which she might never climb back out. But when, actually, had she begun working as a prostitute? Had she dallied in prostitution while living at home with her mother? Or had Belle entered the life after Sarah's death, when it seemed she had nowhere to turn? Belle's biographer, Thompson, identified December 24, 1879, as the night Belle entered the trade. Nineteen at the time, she went to work for a madam named Jennie Hill. However, the attempted suicide suggests that Belle had been working as a prostitute for some time before this.[33]

Jennie Hill, thirty-three years old when Belle showed up at her door in 1879, ran a popular bawdy house in a building that had seen quite a bit of history during better days.[34] The house had been home to Mary Todd before she moved to Illinois, where she met her future husband, Abraham Lincoln. The brick building at the corner of Main and Merino streets dated to the early 1800s and once had served as an inn known as the Sign of the Green Tree. Yet like much of the west end so familiar to Belle, the house had fallen into decline. Now it was a brothel, perhaps the most popular house of prostitution in Lexington. Going to work at Jennie Hill's house marked a major turning point for Belle. When she stepped into that house, Belle left the streets. She had just made a major career move, one that would take her far.

At age nineteen, Belle was the second-youngest woman working at Jennie Hill's. The oldest, Sue Bennett, was forty-five. Other than an eighteen-year-old, the other prostitutes were in their twenties. An African American domestic, aged seventeen, also lived there.

Why Belle left North Upper Street to join Jennie Hill's household is unknown. Was she trying to escape an abusive boyfriend? Did she think she could make more money working in Jennie Hill's "respectable" establishment? Important men in Lexington held Jennie Hill's house of prostitution in high regard. While doing business with these men, Belle would have begun making the acquaintance of bankers, politicians, businessmen, and of course, horsemen. She must have made a decision in going to Jennie Hill's that if she could not abandon the prostitute's life, she would turn it around to her benefit. She would learn how to dress respectably. She would acquire style, good diction, and manners. She would use men to her advantage. If she had been taking morphine or other drugs regularly, she may have curbed her habit. Belle was a woman on the move. She was transforming herself into a businesswoman whose business was men. She was becoming more polished with each month she spent under Jennie Hill's roof. Never would she look back to the streets.

Perhaps it was during Belle's time with Jennie Hill that she began attending horse races. The Kentucky Association track had at last recovered from the Civil War years, that unfortunate time when few stables remained in the region and the U.S. Army had built an earthen fort at the top of the homestretch. In 1872, the association widened the homestretch from forty feet to seventy and built a new wooden grandstand and new stands to accommodate the official timer and judges. The association held two meets annually, in May and September. Purses averaged $300 except for marquee events such as the Phoenix Stakes, named in honor of the popular hotel. When Lexington filled with horsemen and gamblers for the race meets, "the common theme has been the horse— horse for breakfast, horse for dinner and horse for supper.... It is Kentucky's pet carnival."[35]

People walked to the track or rode in public conveyances, and "at an early hour, Lexington was all bustle and excitement" as race fans left the major hotels to arrive at the track well before the noon post time. At times the condition of Lexington streets irritated racegoers, as in 1873 when someone noted the dry and dusty condition of those leading to the track. This was in a September of particularly intense heat, comparable to the hot temperatures more typical of July. The following year, 1874, the hot and dry weather during the autumn meet caused the track to be covered in dust almost four inches deep, slowing the times in the races. The fans did not seem to mind, though, for attendance was high. Women sat in a separate grandstand—a "gilded cage," someone called it.[36] Conventions of the times would have disapproved of decent women mingling at the track with men.

In 1880, getting to the track got easier, at least briefly. An omnibus pulled by horses was Lexington's first attempt at public transportation. Within six months, however, the omnibus company went bankrupt. Racegoers would not see public transportation to the track available again until mule cars went into service in 1882. Until then, spectators walked or rode to the racetrack in a hack or a private conveyance. Hacks were expensive to hire, so many people walked.[37]

Henry "Hal" Price McGrath would mark the start of the spring and fall race meets with a dinner given at his McGrathiana Farm on the Newtown Pike. He had inaugurated these semiannual dinners long before he won the inaugural Kentucky Derby with Aristides in 1875, sending out invitations from an expansive guest list that included politicians, horsemen, and other notables from around the country. In 1871, these included former Kentucky governor James F. Robinson and local horse breeders and racetrack patrons General Abe Buford, owner of Bosque Bonita Farm; General John C. Breckinridge, former vice president of the United States, Confederate secretary of war, and later, acting president of the racecourse; William Cassius Goodloe, a horseman from a large landowning family in Fayette County; and banker James A. Grinstead. One partygoer remarked, "The burgoo actually could not be beat. The wines and liquors were, of course, the best the market affords." The primary conversation, quite naturally, concerned the races.[38]

People liked their racing at the Kentucky Association track. But nothing was perfect, and the patrons had to suffer the annoyance of the hill on the homestretch turn that blocked the horses from the crowd's view. Folks in the grandstand complained about what they couldn't see during this portion of the race, but the horses had it worse. They had to struggle uphill on this portion of the course, and it caused many a likely winner to lose a race. The association cut away at the hill more than once through the years, trying to level it with the remainder of the course.

Across town, the trotting horse races held no less interest for the people of Lexington. During the 1870s, trotters had grown so tremendously popular in the Bluegrass that the *Spirit of the Times* felt the need to reassure Thoroughbred breeders. "The thoroughbred horse of the blue-grass country has not at all depreciated since the breeders of that region began to raise trotters as well."[39] But some were not so sure.

Trotting races had been held since 1859 at the old fairgrounds (also called the city park) on what is now the north campus of the University of Kentucky on a track constructed by Robert Aitcheson Alexander of Woodburn Farm. The sport did not persist through the Civil War in Lexington in any organized fashion because the armies of both the North and South had bivouacked on the fairgrounds. By 1875, Alexander was offering the land for sale. The sport experienced a revival in 1872 when a race meet took place at the home of the Thoroughbreds, the Kentucky Association track. A local newspaper reported that a harness meet transpired at this course without betting and "the straight-laced Methodist mingled in blissful harmony with the less pious reinsman. Everybody was sober and orderly and everything passed off pleasantly."

That was a good thing for the future of the sport. With everyone behaving well, trotting racing was off to a flying start. In 1875, the same year that Churchill Downs inaugurated the Kentucky Derby, the trotters in Lexington moved to the new fairgrounds on South Broadway, a site that has existed into modern times as the Red Mile harness track. The newly organized Kentucky Trotting Horse Breeders Association operated the race meets, leasing the grounds and grandstand from the Agricultural and Mechanical Fair Association. Breckenridge lent his leadership and was among the original stockholders. Other prominent landowners and horsemen served as directors of the trotting association.[40]

Men from the powerful racing and the trotting worlds would come to know Belle quite well, for a web of connections was forming at Jennie Hill's place that would tie Belle closely to these influential drivers of central Kentucky's economy.

chapter FIVE

Networks of Power

In 1880, Belle had begun thinking about opening her own brothel on North Upper Street. Her plans began taking shape in the same year that a Kentucky-bred Thoroughbred named Hindoo took the racing world by storm. Hindoo ran up a string of seven winning races in Lexington, Louisville, St. Louis, and Chicago before his Woodford County owner and breeder, Dan Swigert, took him to New York. He sold him at Saratoga for $15,000, an astonishing sum at the time. Swigert put this money and an additional $15,000 he had received in a horse deal two years earlier toward buying farmland in north Lexington. He called his new farm Elmendorf. This farm, later owned by mining king James Ben Ali Haggin, would become anathema to Belle. Her career would collide head-on with the social reform aims of the man who managed Elmendorf for Haggin. But for now, central Kentucky was talking only of Hindoo and Swigert's good fortune.[1]

Hindoo signaled the advance of a new era in central Kentucky. The Bluegrass had produced quality Thoroughbreds for generations, but the region had yet to be discovered by the big-money men from beyond Kentucky who were getting into racing. This new demographic had emerged as the center of Thoroughbred racing shifted with the Civil War from the South to New York. Industrialists, mining kings, and Wall Street capitalists who had no interest in Kentucky now dominated the game. They built stunning horse farms in the Northeast even as Bluegrass horse breeders struggled to recover financially from the war. With the exception of Swigert and his former employer, Woodburn Farm, no one was getting rich off horses in the Bluegrass. The average Bluegrass breeder realized only a couple hundred dollars for any individual horse sold at auction.

The Bluegrass economy took off after these industrialists, financiers, and mining kings began buying up Kentucky land in the 1890s and early 1900s to turn into Thoroughbred horse farms. Belle's notoriety grew in lockstep with this expansion of Lexington's Thoroughbred business as she began making her reputation with a wider community of horsemen. But during the 1880s, while operating brothels on North Upper Street, she was still a local gal.

Belle quit Jennie Hill to open her first house in July 1881 at 163 North Upper Street. Belle's unit was part of a row house on the east side of the street, near the Transylvania University campus between East Third and East Fourth streets. She required furnishings for her business. On July 8, she took out a mortgage with Brower & Scott, a carpet dealer at 9 West Main Street, for $166 at 6 percent interest in order to purchase 147 yards of Brussels carpet, 80 yards of Ingrain carpet, 2 cornice poles, 7 cornices, 160 yards of lining, 1½ dozen stair rods, 1½ dozen stair pads, 2 Brussels rugs, 5 pairs of curtains, 160 yards of lining, 32 yards of muslin curtains, and 10 red shades and fixtures. Thompson suggested that the number of stair pads and rods that Belle purchased indicated she was using more than one unit in the two-story building. The row houses, their street numbers later changed to 312–316 North Upper Street, were purchased by Transylvania University in 1994 and converted into women's locker room facilities to serve an adjacent athletic field.[2]

Three days later, Belle took out another mortgage, this one for $491.50, to be paid off at $40 monthly beginning September 10, 1881. The mortgage was with Sutton & Son, a furniture dealer at 61 East Main Street, in order to purchase "one fine French dresser suit[e] of furniture, another like suit of furniture, three dressing case suits of furniture, one parlor suit of furniture, one pier glass, one dozen chairs, one-half dozen chairs, three wardrobes, one sofa, one eight-foot table, four mattresses, five sets of springs, one portable set of springs, one pair of sham pillows, and six bolsters."[3] Belle saw to the decorating of her new place and opened for business. We do not know if Jennie Hill wished her well.

Some men might have walked to Belle's new place. But most of her visitors probably hired a horse-drawn cab, or hack, from a line always parked on Main Street across from the Phoenix Hotel. The hotel, billed as the "headquarters for horsemen," sat in a choice spot at the southeast intersection of Main and Mulberry (Limestone) streets, conveniently situated for visitors who wished to make a trip to the houses of Jennie Hill or Belle Brezing. Some Lexington boosters in the 1880s likened the Phoenix to two great southern hotels of the day, the St. Charles in New Orleans and the Kimball House in Atlanta. Such comparisons were probably exaggerations, but a little name-dropping never hurt.[4]

One version or another of the Phoenix Hotel had occupied this strategic corner since 1797, five years after statehood, when Postlethwait's Tavern opened for business. Stagecoach travelers and folks on horseback were among the earliest guests before construction of the railroad that ran past the rear of the hotel. The guest registry had included some of American history's famous characters: Aaron Burr, James Monroe, Andrew Jackson, William Henry Harrison, Ulysses S. Grant, Chester E. Arthur, the Mexican general Santa Anna, and General George Armstrong Custer. Custer took a midday meal at the Phoenix in 1871, compliments of municipal promoters, while on a visit as their guest to view Bluegrass horse farms. The Thoroughbred that Custer acquired in central Kentucky, named Victory, or Vic, as the general called him, would be the horse he rode into battle at the Little Bighorn River in 1876.[5]

By the time Belle set out to open her own business on North Upper Street in 1881, the hotel had risen, like its fabled namesake, from the ashes—and not for the first time. The most recent fires had occurred in 1876 and 1879. An earlier fire destroyed the hotel in 1820, and it had been this particular resurrection from the embers that gave the Phoenix its name.[6]

Networks of connections established at the Phoenix Hotel led to big-money deals in the Bluegrass. These connections intersected with the most powerful group to establish headquarters at the Phoenix: the Lexington Club, founded in 1860. An elite social club, similar to the Pendennis Club in Louisville and the Queen City Club in Cincinnati, the Lexington Club included among its members numerous horsemen such as Catesby Woodford and Colonel Zeke Clay, both landowners in nearby Bourbon County, and the jovial Henry Price McGrath, a former gambling house entrepreneur and now the squire of McGrathiana Farm. Portraits of McGrath and Woodford may have been among those lost when the club rooms burned with the rest of the hotel in 1879. Despite the fire, the club endured. Nearly all the most socially accepted businessmen, horsemen, and politicians belonged to this club, and in 1880 they included Captain Thomas J. Bush, Judge Ben F. Buckner, Major John S. Clark, General William Preston, and former Kentucky governor James F. Robinson. Members of similar clubs in other cities were welcome at the Lexington Club's rooms whenever they visited the city. When Congress adjourned and its members returned to Lexington, these elected representatives frequented the Lexington Club rooms, Senators James B. Beck and Joseph Blackburn among them. The clubrooms became especially popular during the spring and fall races when prominent men from outside Lexington received ten-day guest cards. Colonel Louis Clark, the president of Churchill Downs, frequented the Lexington Club rooms during the races. So did Henry Watterson of Louisville, newspaper editor and proponent of an industrialized "New South." Still another guest was the prizefighter John L. Sullivan.[7]

McGrath, while in attendance, observed a sense of decorum that might have seemed strangely contradictory to his penchant for gambling. But while at the club, McGrath appeared to be restrained. He never participated in card games. In fact, he never wagered against any club member. He was a different man at gambling halls such as the Canfield Casino at Saratoga Springs or at Churchill Downs and other racetracks. When his Aristides won the inaugural Kentucky Derby in 1875, it was said that McGrath took every bet offered to him. He cashed in big, for Aristides had not been the favorite. But at the Lexington Club, McGrath behaved with gentlemanly decorum.[8]

When the Phoenix Hotel reopened in the fall of 1879, the club's headquarters likewise arose from the ashes, its new meeting rooms bearing witness to the usual male conversation concerning horses, politics, and social matters. There was sure to have been a wink here and there about Jennie Hill's place on Main Street and, by 1881, about Belle's popular new place on North Upper Street.

Belle Brezing operated in the shadows, but her house intersected quite neatly with those two spheres of power connected to the Phoenix Hotel: horsemen and the membership of the Lexington Club. Sometimes, the crossover brought Belle's shadow life out into the open, as revealed in an account concerning a well-known man from a respected local family by the name of Stoll. When Lexington Club members needed transportation, they had a habit of instructing a waiter to open a window from their clubrooms on the second floor and yell across the street to the horse-drawn hacks. These cabs, which operated all night, were called "night hawks." One time, a waiter working in the clubrooms opened a window and shouted to a hack driver: "Bradford, Bradford! Mr. Stoll called and said come up to Miss Belle's and pick him up *right now!*"[9]

The Lexington Club was powerful and exclusive, and members ensured that their insular group would remain so by blackballing any prospective member who failed to meet the club's approval. All it took was one "no," and a nominee was out. At the club's annual dinner, generally held three or four days after Christmas, each member was permitted one guest who might be considered suitable for membership. In full evening attire, the men gathered in the main hall and walked two by two into the dining room.[10]

Perhaps it was the Lexington Club's exclusivity that spurred the formation of a rival club in 1886. Resentment over being blackballed may have pulled some men about town into the new Lafayette Club. Its membership included Charles H. Berryman, the man who one day would manage the estate Elmendorf Farm for James Ben Ali Haggin and who would be Belle's adversary. Another who joined the Lafayette Club was Eph Sayre, a regular client at Belle's place. Eventually he would take as his mistress one of Belle's prostitutes, Clara Kessler. (She changed her name to Clara Sayre while working for Belle.) The Lafayette Club first met in the Henry Clay Hotel but soon moved its headquarters to the Navarre Café on the north side of Main Street. An internationally known gambler named Riley Grannan, born in Paris, Kentucky, owned and operated the Navarre Café. He was a close friend of Belle Brezing.[11]

The existence of two rival clubs in this small city did not prove beneficial to the membership of either. Consequently, by 1888, the two clubs combined under the name Lexington Union Club. More widely recognized horsemen joined the group, including Major Thomas C. McDowell, distiller and horse owner James E. Pepper, and W. E. Simms and E. F. Simms, both well known in the trotting horse world. In 1891, a new group called the Turf Club organized, bringing more prominent horsemen into its fold. These included Milton Young, George Denny Jr., B. J. Treacy, Julius Marks, James Straus, S. C. Lyne, and James C. Murphy.[12] In 1892, Marks sent a letter of thanks to women who had presented the Turf Club with a Dresden clock, along with ornaments and vases, presumably for use in the clubrooms. Addressing the letter to Mesdames B. J. Treacy, Thomas Calvert, W. S. Barnes, Joseph Bryan, and others, he wrote rather tongue-in-cheek, for quite possibly the members' wives had been questioning their husbands' whereabouts during the evenings:

> I assure you, proud as we are of our new quarters, with their appointments so highly spoken of by all who have seen them, there is nothing in them so highly appreciated by us as your elegant gift, not so much because of its beauty and intrinsic value, but on account of the fair donors who so handsomely remembered us.
>
> Some vile wretch has insinuated that you selected a clock as a "house present" with "malice aforethought," so that its musical chimes, at certain hours of the night, might remind us that "there is a light in the window" for us at home, and somebody waiting for us there. But we repel, with the indignation which it deserves, such a mean slander.
>
> We know your only aim was to please us and to beautify the rooms in which your husbands take so much pride.
>
> There are doubtless many things we do, which our wives do not approve of. . . .
>
> But when our helpmates join hands with us, and thus stamp their seal of approval on our actions, it affords us a particular and peculiar pleasure, and we feel, indeed, that fortune smiles upon us, and we experience the grateful satisfaction that our efforts to establish the handsomest club house in Kentucky—to which we need not be ashamed to take our wives whenever the "spirit moves" them to accompany us—have not been futile nor selfish. And on such occasions, when you are with us, and when time takes wings on to itself and flies all too fast, you may then point to the

pretty clock on the mantel, and gently whisper in our ears that "it is time to go home."

To Mrs. Joseph Bryant, especially, are we much indebted for the deep interest manifested by her for our club, and the pleasure your nice remembrance gives us.

In the hope that we shall enjoy many happy hours in our new rooms in the company of our wives, and that the clock may never go too fast, I am, dear ladies,

Very respectfully,

Your obedient servant.

Julius Marks, Secy.[13]

What in particular had instigated the wives' concerns about their husbands' evening activities? We can only speculate. But among the men of Lexington, it was no secret that the webs of power they wove intersected with Belle Brezing and her colleagues.

Bernard "B. J." Treacy, whose wife was among the group presenting the gift to the Turf Club, ranked among Lexington's best-known residents. He and his partner, G. D. Wilson, operated a business encompassing horse sales, horse training, and livery stable rentals. Their barn took up an entire block between North Mulberry (Limestone) and Walnut (now Martin Luther King) streets. This facility dated to 1879 and was known as Treacy & Wilson. Its features included 250 stalls constructed within the two-and-a-half-story building. The partners advertised their stables as well ventilated, with an ample water supply and regulated light as well as a high ceiling. Generally they kept three hundred horses of all types and breeds, in particular trotters, Thoroughbreds, and American Saddlebreds. They served an international market. As much as $500,000 circulated annually through their business which, as the partners pointed out, found its way into the economy of the city.[14]

Treacy brokered power connections among horsemen, businessmen, and municipal government. He served on the city council and stood at the center of a big imbroglio after someone accused the city of overpaying for a fire horse in 1880. Treacy & Wilson had billed the city $250 for purchase of this horse, intended to pull a fire wagon; the city later discovered that the horse's owner had priced the horse at $200. A furor arose in council chambers.

A fire horse constituted a significant acquisition for any municipality. During the 1880s, no other way existed to haul firefighting equipment to the scene of a fire. One important attribute of any fire horse was a calm and obliging disposition. A stupid or high-strung animal that would balk before the engine could be hitched would cost firefighters valuable time in reaching the fire. Big, clumsy horses did not suit. Fire horses needed to be fast and strong, about sixteen hands high, weighing from 1,200 to 1,450 pounds, and from four to six years old. At New York's school for fire horses, trainers taught the animals to hurry into position at the front of the engine the minute they heard the gong. A good fire horse in New York went for about $300.[15]

Treacy defended himself by saying the horse he acquired for Lexington was worth $300. He insisted he did not want the city council to think Treacy & Wilson had brokered a horse that was not worth every penny paid for it. He informed the council that he reserved the right to make a profit on any horse he sold. City council members mulled over the matter in their chambers, typically thick with tobacco smoke "which hung like a cloud over the desks."[16]

The city council's meeting room, as Treacy knew, was a clubby emporium, not unlike the Lexington Club rooms, the Turf Club's headquarters, or perhaps, Belle Brezing's parlor. On one evening when council members were to convene for a caucus, the one who arrived first awaited the others with a "big bellied" bottle of ten-year-old bourbon flanked by bottles of champagne (Mumm's Extra Dry). Setting the bottles on a table, he sat with his legs across the back of a chair.[17] His relaxed manner and the beverages of choice indicate that council business was largely an informal affair attended by men whose sociability would improve with free-flowing spirits. The relaxed atmosphere belied the power these men possessed to determine the course of the city.

Council members dealt with those they disagreed with in a curious way. One Sunday morning in 1881, early churchgoers spied an effigy hanging twenty feet high on a telephone pole on the courthouse side of the Cheapside square. The figure had two faces, representing Janus, the mythical character who looks deceptively forward and backward simultaneously. The good citizens of Lexington recognized right away the likeness to a particular city councilman. The newspaper noted, "A gentleman who claimed to have seen many such effigies, said to our reporter that this one was gotten up in the best style of any he had ever seen." When firemen removed the effigy, its clothes were given to charity and the straw stuffing given to cows. Treacy was also at the center of this disagreement, whatever its source. He engaged another councilman in a shouting match in chambers, and when the two moved their fight out to the hallway, he chased his opponent with an open pocketknife.[18] This was the way Lexington operated in the 1880s when Belle Brezing was building her business.

Belle turned her rented quarters at 163 North Upper Street into the most fashionable place she could afford. In the beginning, she paid her bills promptly. By December 30, 1881, she had paid off the mortgage taken out on July 8 with Brower & Scott. In February 1882, she paid off the mortgage with Sutton & Son. The following month, Belle purchased additional furniture from Sutton & Son, paying $1 in cash and signing a note for $429.95. She would not pay off this note for three more years, in October 1885.[19]

In 1883 Belle purchased a house further north in the same block, three houses down from the intersection of East Fourth Street. On July 18, she paid $825 for this house at 194 North Upper Street, the brothel she would occupy for the next six years. She put $400 down in cash and took out a mortgage for the remaining $425, with the note due in 12 months at 8 percent interest.[20]

By this time, Belle had friends in high places. In December 1882, she was indicted for "keeping a bawdy house" (her first but not her last such indictment). Five months before she purchased 194 North Upper Street, on February 7, 1883, Belle's friends came to her rescue: she received a pardon from Kentucky governor Luke Blackburn.[21]

A Lexington policewoman, Margaret Egbert, recalled walking with some friends past 194 North Upper Street and seeing a party going strong at Belle's house. The prostitutes wore evening gowns, and the men were also in evening dress. Belle had always been well dressed, according to Egbert. She knew Belle fairly well, for the two had attended Dudley School at the same time. Egbert also remembered seeing Belle as a teenager after the death of Belle's mother when Belle lived on South Mill Street between Maxwell and High streets. "She was a beautiful girl and wore handsome clothes," Egbert related, but "was regarded as being not a nice girl."[22] Egbert would encounter Belle again when she later worked as a "policewoman."

The house on North Upper Street attracted an older, established clientele along with a younger demographic. One winter night, four young men brought their horse-drawn sleigh around to Belle's, calling to the prostitutes to come out for a ride. The men drove the horses as fast as they could run through the snow, going as far as the first toll-gate house on the Paris Turnpike. At the tollgate, the driver whirled the horses quickly around and turned the sleigh over on its side. All the passengers fell out. The young men righted the sleigh, but they drove off without the prostitutes, leaving the young women to walk back to Belle's. The walk was a long one on a cold winter's night.[23]

Belle's business had started off well. But five months after moving to 194 North Upper, she appears to have come up short of cash. She mortgaged the house in December for $927.93 to William and John Williamson. The terms were $463.96, payable in six months at 6 percent interest, with the remaining $463.97 due in twelve months at the same interest rate. She paid off the loan November 24, 1884. She took out another loan, this one for $1,000 secured against 194 North Upper, on March 18, 1885. Asa Dodge held this mortgage. Belle paid off the loan March 18, 1886. She mortgaged 194 North Upper Street twice more for cash, for $922 on May 1, 1885, and for $1,000 on July 23, 1886. Additionally, she mortgaged the carpets, oilcloths, curtains, and cornices in this house in June 1885 for $921.85 cash.[24]

Whatever Belle's financial troubles had been, she appeared in far better circumstances by October 1886, when she paid $1,700 cash for a house on West Fourth Street between Kenton and Campbell streets. In November 1888, Belle bought a house on Dewees Street, paying $2,500 in cash.[25] No evidence exists that Belle lived in either house. But her ability to pay cash for real estate indicates that her finances had improved.

The indictments against Belle that had begun in December 1882 were occurring more frequently. From 1882 through 1903, Fayette County grand juries would indict Belle at least once a year and sometimes more often. After 1910, the indictments began again. The first indictment, in 1882, for "keeping a bawdy house," described the frivolity taking place at Belle's. Witnesses had seen Belle "habitually induce men and women of evil name and fame to frequent said house . . . making indecent exposures of their persons, using profane, vulgar and obscene language, and engaging in other acts of lewdness to the common nuisance and annoyance of good citizens of the Commonwealth of Kentucky and especially those living in the neighborhood of said house." Belle deposited $250 with the trustee of the jury in lieu of paying bail.[26] Two months later, Governor Blackburn pardoned her. The unanswered question is why Blackburn took an interest in Belle's case.

A similar incident occurred in 1888, when some of Lexington's most powerful men took up the defense of a brothel keeper named Sue Green. A grand jury had indicted her for operating a "house of prostitution" on Megowan Street. Soon afterward, a flight of letters arrived on the desk of Kentucky governor Simon Buckner demanding justice for Green. Commonwealth's attorney C. J. Bronston wrote to the governor on Phoenix Hotel stationery, refusing to grant validity to the complaint against Green because the complainants were "negroes" inhabiting the red-light district. The Fayette County sheriff, J. C. Rogers, sent Green to the governor with a letter seeking her pardon. Sheriff Rogers explained that the woman's house was mortgaged and she bore the expense of caring for her family. A Fayette County judge, S. G. Sharp, also wrote the governor, insisting Green should be pardoned because she operated her business within the confines of the red-light district. Green's attorney, E. L. Hutchinson, also wrote a letter on her behalf.[27]

Indictments brought against Belle throughout the 1880s generally originated with complaints from a group of neighbors determined to run her out of North Upper Street. These people included Rev. F. M. Hurst, 227 North Upper; William Masner, a grocer whose home was at his business at 205 North Upper; Letcher Lusby, 11 East Fourth; B. M. Williams, a confectioner living at his business at 117 North Limestone; W. W. Monroe, 193 North Limestone; George W. Didlake, 197 North Limestone; Charles Allen, a grocer at 182 North Upper; Stephen Dunn, 146 West Fourth; and women including a Mrs. Jones, Mrs. M. Brookins, Mrs. Sue Patterson, Mrs. Francis Elliston, Mrs. Emma Gray, and Mrs. Lynch.[28]

Perhaps Belle should have worked harder at getting along with her neighbors. But she was not the only Lexington brothel keeper indicted in the 1880s. The grand juries even indicted men who owned properties named in prostitution cases. A grand jury in 1886 indicted James Cox on a charge of "nuisance," accusing him of leasing a building to one Mattie Watkins when he knew the building would be used for prostitution.[29] Neighborhoods had begun to organize resistance to brothels, or at least they cooperated with grand juries by serving as witnesses.

By the late 1880s, Belle's neighbors acquired a valuable ally in their bid to rid North Upper Street of prostitution. This was Charles Moore, a former minister of a church in Versailles who had lost his religion, left the church, and now proclaimed himself to be an infidel but an infidel driven by conservative morality. He was an odd sort, a real iconoclast. Born into the Bluegrass aristocracy of wealthy landowners and horse owners, he "lampooned" the local elites, whom he considered to be dilettantes, according to his biographer, John Sparks.[30] Moving to Lexington, Moore took a job in journalism and began to assail liquor, tobacco, and horseracing. In central Kentucky, choosing to fight these particular elements was like tilting at windmills. But Moore persevered.

Moore's resignation from his pastorate in Versailles had caused quite a commotion in that community. But Moore had only begun. Removed to Lexington, Moore switched back and forth between reporting jobs at two newspapers, the *Observer* and the *Transcript*. He would get fired at one newspaper and go to the other, back and forth. The problem was the abrasive attacks he leveled at everything the locals held dear. Readers complained. Editors eventually began to edit his copy heavily—or to decline to print his stories. Moore felt outraged. He believed his editors were pandering to saloon owners because they kept his reports of saloon fights out of their newspapers. Weary of interference, Moore started his own newspaper in 1884, the *Blue Grass Blade*. Like Moore himself, the *Blade* was outrageous and highly controversial. Sparks suggested this made the *Blade* the most widely read paper in Kentucky. You never knew what Moore was going to write or how he was going to say it. You also never knew if he printed the truth.[31]

The *Blade* gave Moore a sense of power and provided him a forum free from editorial interference. He wrote that his former employer, the *Lexington Transcript,* was an "organ of Presbyterianism, Catholicism, whiskey, and Democracy"—an odd combination—and that the newspaper's owner had taken a saloonkeeper's bribe to help fund his candidacy for mayor. Statements like this eventually landed Moore in jail for libel.[32] Moore's other pet projects included the banishment of prostitution, gambling, and alcohol. He believed liquor to be as destructive to happiness as another target of his iconoclasm, Christianity.

Given his family ties, Moore would have been expected to own Thoroughbred racehorses. But he did not. He associated the sport with gambling. On the other hand, he owned trotters. He did not view the trotting sport as intrinsically evil because trotters could lead double lives as road horses. Therefore, trotters were as wholesome as the American flag. In 1889, Moore purchased two trotting fillies at a dispersal of trotters at the Fairlawn Farm near Lexington (near what is now the northeast intersection of North Broadway with Loudon). He paid $700 for a yearling filly and $650 for a weanling.[33]

Moore targeted Belle increasingly through the latter 1880s. But he was not her only problem. On July 13, 1882, she gave birth to a stillborn child. The infant was buried at Lexington Cemetery. Another problem emerged concerning Daisy May's future. Belle never lost contact with Mrs. Barnett while this woman on West Main Street cared for her daughter. But by the time Daisy May reached age six, both women began to realize the girl was not like others her age; they believed she was "retarded." One Lexington resident, Tandy Hughes, said Belle "did not know anything was wrong with the child mentally until she started to school." Belle sent Daisy May to live with Catholic nuns in Newport, Kentucky, at a school for children like her. She enrolled her daughter under the name of Daisy Barnett.[34]

Despite money problems during the early 1880s, Belle's business at 194 North Upper Street eventually improved. Her ledger pages reveal how much Belle charged her prostitutes for board. For example, a prostitute named Ida Martin paid Belle $16 weekly, broken down into daily increments generally noted as $3 or $5. Belle was housing five prostitutes: Ida, Mattie, Blanch, Gertie, and Susie. Charges for their board would have grossed $80 weekly for Belle, or $320 each month. But this was not clear money for Belle. She had to pay for a cook to feed these women. She had to buy coal oil. Occasionally, she replaced the bedsheets and towels. She even noted a small expense for birdseed, for like most brothel keepers, she kept a parrot.[35]

Another part of Belle's income came from the sale of beer and wine. She noted a $50 charge to Will Sayre for wine. Billy Mabon purchased two bottles of alcohol for $5.50. On pages torn from an undated ledger, the names of Will and Eph Sayre appear multiple times, the two of them running up charges for beer. The surname Chinn appears next to a $5 charge for wine.[36] Not a penny came in or out of her house without Belle making note in her books.

The ebb and flow of Belle's business peaked with the race meets held every spring and fall and fair week held during the summer. In May 1883 the newspaper noted, "A ball at Miss Belle Breezing's, which will come off during the races, will probably be pretty breezy, and the proprietress will be the Belle of the ball. A large attendance is anticipated. Our reporter will be provided with a telephone and telescope, and will take it in from the top of Morrison College." Undoubtedly the newspaper published this item as a hoax but one with a partial grounding in the facts, for it reveals that the community recognized that Belle assumed a greater presence during the races. The headline read: "Bal de Demi-monde." Belle clearly recognized the value of race week to her business. She wrote "race week" next to entries in her account book for 1887. She charged one of her prostitutes $5.50 on Sunday of that race week, indicating that Belle slightly increased her charges for board when the horses were in town.[37]

Mabon, whose purchase of alcohol was noted in Belle's 1883 account book, was believed by everyone to be her lover. He certainly acted like her lover, and he enjoyed extraordinary privileges in her house. He had come into Belle's life perhaps as early as her teenage years. Belle's good friend Pink Thomas recalled, "She said she had her child when she was about 16 years old and it was after that that she met Billy and he set her up in business." Mabon's feelings for Belle were clear. He presented her with a variety of gifts through the years, sometimes inscribing them "Kitten," his pet name for her.[38]

Mabon was well connected. His sister, Alice Morgan, who was married to R. C. Morgan, lived at 408 West Third Street, a fashionable address. The community knew Mabon as a bookkeeper who never remained long at any place of employment. Before meeting Belle, he had worked as a clerk at 10 North Broadway during 1875 and 1876. In 1877 and 1878, he earned his living as a "collector." In 1881, while Belle still worked at Jennie Hill's house, Mabon held a job as a clerk at 19 East Main Street, keeping that job into 1882. From 1883 through 1887, he worked as a bookkeeper at the National Exchange Bank, boarding at 58 North Upper Street, not far from Belle. The following year, Mabon appeared to be self-employed. In 1890, he "clerked" for the Lexington Brick Co. on East Main Street and had moved his residence to 46 East Second Street.[39] By 1902, he would hold a bookkeeping job with the Lexington Water Works.

As Belle and Mabon grew closer, they stepped out as a couple in public. The two must have made for quite a sight when Mabon escorted Belle on drives through town in a horse-drawn conveyance. The good citizens easily recognized Belle. Lexington was small enough at the time that it was hard to live an anonymous life.

At one time, Belle took great pleasure in riding her own horse sidesaddle through town. Her chestnut-colored stallion was handsome and high spirited. Belle must have been quite a good rider to be able to handle such a strong-willed horse. But one day in May 1883, when she was riding down Main Street amid crowds celebrating the May Day holiday, two small boys inadvertently startled the horse, which bolted. Belle's horsemanship was evident for all to see as she managed to keep her seat, controlling the horse and preventing him from running away. But the horse, thrown off balance, fell, rolling over on Belle. She lay unconscious for several hours. The doctor feared for her life. A few nights later, however, Belle had recovered and was back in charge of her house. In small and gossipy Lexington, the horse accident made the newspaper.[40]

Belle did not ride about town on horseback again after the accident. Instead, she made use of a conveyance known as a phaeton, a horse-drawn vehicle that was the sports car of the nineteenth century. Phaetons were open-air carriages generally pulled by one or two horses. A team of matched chestnut horses pulled Belle's, lending the vehicle an extra sporty appearance. Her driver (called a coachman) was black. He wore the fancy dress of a carriage driver, called livery, which included a tall, black hat. Belle rode in the cushioned seat facing forward, always elegantly dressed.[41]

Belle was not the only resident of a brothel to drive about Lexington in a phaeton. Joseph Tanner recalled that prostitutes paraded through town in this manner, usually one or two of them to a carriage. Some would complete the elegant turnout with the addition of a liveried footman sitting up front with the coachman. Tanner said prostitutes also sauntered about the streets "in a style of dress and walk" that left no doubt about their profession. But those were the lower class of prostitutes who could not afford a carriage ride. Tanner said their class also could be identified by their appearance, "indicating both by face and dress dissipation and degradation." The brothel owners and the better class of prostitutes cut a dash in their horse-drawn vehicles, drawing stares from the townsfolk.[42]

Charles Moore, thorn in the side of Lexington liquor and horse racing interests, remained a local force. Unable to succeed at banning alcohol or Thoroughbreds from Lexington, he began to aim his fury at three brothels operating on North Upper Street: Belle's place at no. 194; Lettie Powell's, next door at 196 North Upper; and Molly Parker's, farther south in the block at no. 154. In the year 1889, the elements of a perfect storm came together for Moore.

When the *Lexington Daily Press* reached the streets on January 12, 1889, the newspaper carried a story about citizens demanding that the city close these brothels. Charles Moore's name led a list of thirty-three people who had signed a petition seeking the shutdown. Others who signed included the president of Kentucky University (now Transylvania University), the president of the College of the Bible (now Lexington Theological Seminary), and the superintendent of public schools. Moore and the others complained that the brothels operated in full view of students at Kentucky University, the College of the Bible, and two public schools. But the proximity of the schools might have been no more than an excuse. Sparks, Moore's biographer, offered another possibility that adds a new dimension to Moore's intense focus on these brothels. Moore's brother-in-law, James Cantrill, had served as lieutenant governor during the administration of Governor Luke Blackburn—the same Blackburn who had pardoned Belle Brezing in 1883. Perhaps, wrote Sparks, "it may simply have outraged Charles that his upright, churchgoing, married brother-in-law, other state politicians like Blackburn, and Lexington's city officials could look the other way for the benefit of the town's flesh trade while perhaps simultaneously discreetly sampling the wares that the Upper Street houses had to offer."[43] So true. You never knew who might walk through Belle Brezing's door.

This petition certainly got the attention of the next grand jury called into session, which indicted Belle and the other madams on February 13, 1889, listing the charge as one of "nuisance." Of all the indictments Belle had received beginning in 1882, this one appeared the most ominous. North Upper Street no longer seemed the ideal location for her business. She was ready for a move. By this time a new man had entered her life. Tradition in Lexington holds that he gave Belle $50,000, more than enough to purchase another house and move away from North Upper Street.

Belle learned of a house belonging to Mike Foley for sale at 59 Megowan Street. Foley would not have harbored any moral misgivings about selling to Belle; he already rented some of the houses he owned to madams and prostitutes. Two years earlier, in 1886, a grand jury had indicted Foley on a "nuisance" charge, accusing him of "being the owner and controller of a certain house" leased to one Susie Lillie. The indictment charged that Foley knew Lillie would use the house for prostitution.[44]

When Belle expressed interest in 59 Megowan, Foley agreed to sell to her. John J. Bruce had sold this property in 1882 to Mary Foley, Mike Foley's wife, for $300 cash and two promissory notes, both for $200. Belle would acquire the house and grounds for $1,400 cash.

On Sunday, June 16, 1889, the *Kentucky Leader* ran a notice from Belle informing all that she was departing North Upper Street.

Take Notice

As I am about to move from my present residence, I wish to have all my accounts settled at once. Those having bills against me please call and settle, and those owing me do the same. I am anxious to have all settled at once.

Belle Brezing.[45]

With a new benefactor, a new house, and a rising fame that extended beyond central Kentucky, Belle prepared to depart North Upper Street and step into a new life.

chapter **SIX**

A Wealthy Benefactor

Two brothers from Philadelphia, George and William A. Singerly, inherited an immense estate in 1880. In an indirect way, Belle also benefited from their father's largesse. Joseph Singerly had helped pioneer the street railroad system in Philadelphia. He bequeathed son William more than fourteen thousand shares in the Germantown (Pennsylvania) Passenger Railway Company, a treasure appraised at $705,650, or $16.5 million in 2013 dollars. To George he left a comfortable inheritance locked in an annuity that enabled George to live a self-indulgent lifestyle.

Either Joseph preferred William to his younger brother, or he recognized William as the better businessman of the two. Some years earlier, William had assisted his father in managing the streetcar line. He then moved to Chicago, where he worked for himself in commodities. He returned to Philadelphia when his father asked him to manage the Germantown Railway, proving himself quite capable in business by expanding the system. William eventually realized a huge profit by selling his shares for approximately double their original value, $1.5 million.

But William did not rest on his riches. In 1877, he purchased a lackluster newspaper, the *Public Record*. He did not know much about the publishing business, but he saw the opportunities. He made improvements and changed the name in 1879 to the *Philadelphia Record*. He boosted circulation until the *Record* emerged as a leader among morning papers in that city. He was a hard man in business, typical of the industrialists and capitalists of his time. When unionized compositors, or printers, went on strike shortly before Christmas in 1891, Singerly stood alone among Philadelphia's newspaper publishers in refusing to accede to their demands for a better standard of living. He brought in nonunion workers to put out the next day's paper.[1]

Singerly's business interests were diverse. To supply his newspaper with paper, Singerly bought a pulp mill in Elkton, Maryland. He turned to real estate development and built more than a thousand homes in Philadelphia. He opened a theater. He founded the Chestnut Street National Bank. He was also influential in politics. Reflecting Singerly's Democratic politics, the *Record* assailed corruption in Philadelphia, a daring proposition in a city where Republican bosses owned every inch of lucrative turf, right down to saloons and vice. Pennsylvanians nominated him for governor in 1894, but he lost the election. He did, however, help put Grover Cleveland in the White House in 1885 and again in 1893. The president relaxed occasionally on Singerly's yacht.[2]

Brother George was given the title of manager of the paper mill. He might also have served as an associate sports editor of the *Record*. But to understand George's true calling one has only to read his obituary from 1902: his life consisted almost entirely of a long and successful association with trotters and Thoroughbred racehorses. Unlike William, who married and was widowed twice, George never married. He spent all his energies, and a considerable amount of his fortune, on fast horses. In 1880 he was one of the five charter members who founded Philadelphia's Belmont Driving Club, an elite group of wealthy men who drove their speedy trotters for recreation. (This amusement, done for pleasure, was separated by a wide gulf of class-consciousness from the professional sport of harness racing.) He purchased a trotter in Kentucky, Prince Wilkes, for $300 as a weanling in the early 1880s, eventually selling the horse for $30,000. He bought half interest in a trotting horse farm operation in central Kentucky. He owned a trotting stallion named Messenger Chief, which stood at stud in Versailles, Kentucky. He invented a horseshoe called the Singerly Safety Shoe. He owned a successful Thoroughbred, Han d'Or, son of an esteemed stallion called Hanover, which he sold to another street railway mogul, William Collins Whitney. Besides driving trotters in harness, George rode them to saddle, holding a record for the latter. Among his trotters was a mare he named Pretty Belle, a mare who may have been quite appropriately named. For as it happened, one or both of the Singerly brothers befriended Belle Brezing and became her major benefactor.[3]

George was not merely a wealthy man spending money with abandon on horses. People recognized him for his knowledge of these animals, particularly the trotter that was so in vogue during his lifetime. He did not merely spend money in the horse business; he made money. He was a remarkable judge of what made a good horse, and this was how he ran up his investments when buying and selling trotters, with Prince Wilkes his best example of this skill. People regarded George as an authority on horses. They also knew him as one of the best amateur drivers in the sport.[4]

Precisely when George began traveling to Lexington in search of horses is unclear, although sometime during the 1880s he became a regular at the horse auctions and trotting meets. He thoroughly immersed himself in Bluegrass horse culture. If you wished to speak with this wealthy Philadelphian while he was in Lexington, the easiest way to find him was to poke your head in the door of the tiny office in the Phoenix Hotel rented to William L. "George Wilkes" Simmons. Here pulsed the heartbeat of the Bluegrass horse culture. You weren't anybody in the horse business until you received the blessing of George Wilkes Simmons within his citadel of news and views. (When Simmons made a new acquaintance in his office at the Phoenix Hotel, he often invited him to his Ash Grove Farm on the Frankfort Pike.) Within this little pocket of power, measuring no larger than eight feet by ten, men closely associated with the trotting horse milieu shared gossip and information. George Singerly was among those who visited Simmons.[5]

George Singerly was not the only man of immense wealth to take a seat in Simmons's office. For a good fifteen years before patrons of the Thoroughbred sport would "discover" central Kentucky, a handful of wealthy men in search of trotting stock traveled to Lexington and befriended Simmons. These men were not in Kentucky to buy Bluegrass horse farms. Not yet. Outsiders generally did not begin venturing into Bluegrass real estate until the 1890s, and then only sparingly, for the land rush of capitalists did not begin until the early 1900s. But by the 1880s, wealthy outsiders who fancied owning select trotting horses were beginning to notice that the right Kentucky trotter could speed faster than its eastern counterpart. Simmons entertained Robert Bonner, owner of the *New York Ledger,* along with his well-known son, Allie Bonner. Others to take a seat in Simmons's lair included J. Malcolm Forbes, whose outstanding trotting farm in the East would pay Governor Leland Stanford of California $125,000 for a single breeding stallion, and Marcus Daly who, as owner of the Anaconda Copper Mining Company, was known as the Copper King. Within the confines of this eight-by-ten-foot space, Simmons managed to squeeze not only chairs for men of wealth as well as for ordinary horsemen, but also the piles of horse books, magazines, and trotting guides he collected. The clutter served a purpose. Whenever a dispute arose over a pedigree or a timed record, the parties would convene at Simmons's office to research the answer. It was almost as though a telegraph line of gossip led straight there. No matter where in the Bluegrass someone bought or sold a trotter or pacer (both types became recognized as the Standardbred breed in 1879), information quickly made its way to this little hotspot. The *Morning Herald* in Lexington called this gathering place "the resort of all visiting horsemen" and noted that "men who have made turf history" treated Simmons's office like their private turf club. By frequenting this office, George Singerly became part of the regional trotting horse culture. Kentucky trotters had become a hot commodity, and Singerly secured a place for himself right at the source.[6]

This explosion of popularity for Kentucky trotters in the 1880s marked a complete turnaround from previous decades, when this type of horse had encountered a great degree of opposition when it began to appear in the Bluegrass. Trotters descend partly from the Thoroughbred breed, but in Bluegrass Kentucky, cradle of the Thoroughbred, trotters were clearly unwelcome among their racier cousins. Kentuckians, many descended from Virginians, wanted their horses to fly at a fast gallop, something at which the Thoroughbred excelled. To these expatriate Virginians, horses were something to ride and to race. Trotters (and also pacers), which were light harness horses, did not gallop. They were hitched between the shafts of a buggy and trotted or paced at a slower speed. They were bred and trained to trot in a two-beat gait, moving their legs diagonally: left hind and right front go forward simultaneously, followed by right hind and left front working in unison. Pacers moved in a slightly swaying, side-to-side gait: the right hind and the right front moved forward together, repeated by a similar action on the other side.

Trotters (and even a few pacers) had distinguished themselves since the early 1800s (Lady Suffolk, "the old gray mare," comes to mind, with her 2:29½ mile in 1845). Amateur road driving (as opposed to the professional racing of horses on a track) became popular by 1835, long before a "Standardbred" breed of harness horses evolved. The harness horse's kingdom lay in the North, most notably Orange County, New York, which has been identified as the birthplace of the trotter. New York became the center of road driving, although Boston, Philadelphia, and eventually Cleveland and cities in California followed suit.

Light harness horses eclipsed Thoroughbreds in popularity in the Northeast in large part because churchmen of the evangelical religious traditions did not frown upon harness horses racing at speed. These horses were basically utilitarian horses (at least they were in the beginning), and you could not blame a man for turning on the speed when another man's horse came alongside his on the road. Thoroughbreds had been popular in New York during colonial times, but after about 1830 they had no chance against the waves of religious revival and anti-gambling sentiment that swept through the Northeast. Oneida County was, after all, the center of the "burned-over" district of fiery religious rhetoric and conversions that swept across upstate New York in the early nineteenth century. Thoroughbred racing fell to the ax of religious reformers with the result that, by the later 1840s, only one Thoroughbred stallion stood at stud in New York. Without racing, the market for breeding was nonexistent. The Thoroughbred found its home among Virginians, Kentuckians, Mississippians, Alabamans, and Georgians, who were of a more liberal religious bent that coexisted with the practice of gambling. Southerners had no problem wagering gold, slaves, or even their plantations on a horse race.[7]

Bluegrass Thoroughbred breeders did everything they could to keep the trotter out of Kentucky. Then a son of Henry Clay, James B. Clay, fell in love with trotting horses while on a trip to view shorthorn cattle in Dutchess County, New York, in 1853. He purchased a trotter named Mambrino Chief for $4,000. A handler rode the stallion to the Clay family's Ashland estate, where he arrived on February 21, 1854. Thoroughbred breeders realized they could not ostracize or even openly criticize Clay for bringing a trotter into their midst: because the Clay family was held in high regard for its pioneering involvement in

Thoroughbred racing and breeding, Clay's status was immense in the Bluegrass horse world. The coming of Mambrino Chief to the Bluegrass allowed the trotter a wedge in the door and set Kentucky on a new course.

Two years later, Robert Aitcheson Alexander got into the horse business and began adding not only Thoroughbreds but trotters to his livestock breeding operation at Woodburn Farm. During the Civil War, Alexander suffered an irreparable loss when outlaws twice raided his farm, stealing a trotter named Abdallah on their second raid in February 1865. The raiders abandoned Abdallah in Lawrenceburg, but not before they had ridden him hard, even forcing the horse to swim across the icy Kentucky River. Alexander managed to retrieve Abdallah, but the horse soon contracted pneumonia and died, aged thirteen. One of the foals the stallion had sired before coming to Woodburn Farm, a mare named Goldsmith Maid, would set a new world trotting record seven times. She was immensely popular. Fans turned out to see her race all over the United States, often tearing down fences at the trotting tracks to try to get close enough to touch her. Everyone wondered about the effect that Goldsmith Maid's sire, Abdallah, would have had on the sport if only he hadn't been stolen and killed.[8]

Alexander, like Clay, could ignore the prejudice against trotters in Kentucky because he had attained a status that exceeded even that of the Clay family. Woodburn Farm occupied a virtual pedestal as the leading stock farm in the United States during the 1860s and 1870s. No one was going to question Alexander's choice of horses to stand at stud, for those choices included the renowned Thoroughbred Lexington, which reigned as the No. 1 breeding stallion for sixteen years. Alexander had brought another trotting stallion, Pilot Jr., to Woodburn, and this horse would exert a tremendous influence on trotters through his daughters. Descendants included Jay-Eye-See, the first to trot a mile in 2:10. Another was Maud S., who would beat Jay-Eye-See's record. William Vanderbilt liked the horse so much that he bought her and immediately turned her into a roadster for his private recreation.[9]

For a brief window, perhaps between 1885 and 1915, the Standardbred may have eclipsed the Thoroughbred in popularity everywhere in the United States. Charles Leerhsen made this argument in his biography of the famous Standardbred pacer Dan Patch.[10] This was happening even in the Bluegrass. Lexington's Kentucky Association track was in its dotage and in fact closed down for want of money from 1898 to 1905, until a capitalist from Pennsylvania stepped in and rescued Thoroughbred racing—and potentially the regional breeding industry—by providing the cash to reopen the track. Even worse, Thoroughbred racing was adversely affected by powerful antigambling campaigns in nearly every state in the early 1900s; New York's prestigious tracks shut down entirely from 1910 to 1912. Throughout this time, harness racing enjoyed immense popularity in Lexington and elsewhere. How could you possibly offend reformers by putting down a little bet on a horse that really and truly was utilitarian because it could pinch-hit as family transportation? When the Lexington trotting meet opened each autumn, the trains ran specials to the city, and downtown merchants displayed the race trophies in their storefront windows. Local newspapers devoted a great amount of space to the "trots," and social functions evolved around the meet.[11]

But that lay in the future. The trotter who had captured everyone's attention in Kentucky during the 1870s was George Wilkes, which brings us back to "George Wilkes" Simmons and his den of trotting gossip where George Singerly often visited. A man named William H. Wilson had brought the horse George Wilkes from New York to Kentucky in 1873 while holding a one-year lease on the stallion. (The brothers William L. and Z. E. Simmons of New York had owned the horse during most of his racing career, changing his name at one point to George Wilkes in honor of the editor of a popular sporting weekly based in New York called the *Spirit of the Times*.) By wheeling and dealing, Wilson managed to breed eighty-two mares to the stallion during that one-year lease: quite an achievement, considering the prejudice against trotters. This brought the Simmons brothers to realize that a market for trotters might actually exist in Kentucky, so they moved to the Bluegrass and retook possession of the stallion. Under their handling, George Wilkes exploded in popularity and produced a remarkable line of horses. Everybody wanted one of his offspring. Quite naturally, prices went up. In the midst of Thoroughbred country, George Wilkes was a hot commodity, giving Thoroughbred breeders competition for available stud dollars.[12]

Another offspring of the ill-fated Abdallah was Almont, which

Woodburn Farm sold for $8,000 to Richard West, a young Scott County man starting out in the business. The horse proved highly successful at Edge Hill, the farm West founded near Georgetown. Another farm established at this time was Fairlawn, which a veteran of the Mexican War and the Civil War, General W. T. Withers, created in Lexington (on what is now North Broadway near Loudon Avenue). In 1875, Withers purchased Almont for $15,000. Almont began to draw wide attention while at Fairlawn, attracting visitors such as Ulysses S. Grant after he left the White House. Grant was a superb horseman who loved to drive fast trotters. In New York, he once was cited for exceeding the speed limit behind a fast filly and had to pay a fine. Foreign buyers also began to visit Fairlawn, most notably King Kalakahua of Hawaii. General Withers soon added a horse named Happy Medium to his stallion roster, and this horse would sire trotters that were the rock stars of their era: Pilot Medium and Nancy Hanks.[13]

So George Singerly would have interacted with a cast of characters who favored the trotter when he began visiting Lexington in the 1880s. They included General Withers; Colonel West; Simmons; the horse dealer R. L. Strader, who kept a barn close by the trotting track; and B. J. Treacy, the livery stable owner and city councilman whose trotting horse farm, Ashland Park, stood where the Kenwick subdivision developed along Richmond Road. One more character who would have made Singerly's acquaintance was the wily, controversial, and contrarian veterinarian Dr. Levi Herr. His name would become a household word in horse circles. "If asked who is the best horseman in America, we should unhesitatingly say Dr. L. Herr," proclaimed a correspondent for the *Spirit of the Times* in 1880.[14] But not everyone agreed with the theories and practices of this veterinarian.

Born in Lancaster, Pennsylvania, in 1814, Dr. Herr arrived in Lexington to practice veterinary medicine in 1850 or 1852, a time when Thoroughbred horsemen were still trying to keep the trotter out of Kentucky. In fact, Herr arrived in the Bluegrass shortly before James Clay so daringly imported the trotting stallion Mambrino Chief. Herr began with 135 acres a mile south of the courthouse, along the Nicholasville Pike, and named his estate Forest Park, for the land was then a forest, not the jumble of fast food restaurants and stores that Nicholasville Road has become. Before long he expanded his farm to 300 acres.[15]

Railroad tracks bordered Herr's estate on the west, with the Nicholasville Pike fronting the eastern side. In between these boundaries was an estate of splendid land thick with the bluegrass for which the region is named. Two gates stood at the entrance, about two hundred feet apart. A carriage drive laid in crushed rock, or macadam, led in a half-moon shape from the front of the residence to each gate. Another drive laid in crushed rock led to the stables and the carriage house, both set among shade trees. Herr's trainer, an African American and former Thoroughbred jockey of some renown named Tommy Britton, lived with his family in a cottage near the stables. Within forty yards of the stables lay the trotting track. Herr thought the track resulted in timed miles that were a touch on the slow side, but that was because the turns were tight. He had wanted a track a full mile in circumference, and with the way the forested land lay, his only option was to build short, tight turns.[16] Herr's generosity was boundless to those who loved to drive trotters, many of them amateurs who drove for recreation. He erected a gate to allow access from the Nicholasville Pike for any who desired to drive on his track. From here, visitors enjoyed a splendid view of the forested countryside as well as the city.

Generous though he was with his racetrack and his expertise, Dr. Herr's outspokenness and iconoclastic views put him at odds with many trotting horsemen. In fact, many called him a butcher and a murderer. He initiated the practice of breaking trotters as yearlings; previously, horsemen had waited until the horses were about three years old. You could not argue Herr's success on the track, however. He trained outstanding trotters such as Lady Thorn and Director.[17]

Additional dissension churned over Herr's theories of horse breeding. The Thoroughbred blood that had enabled the refinement in trotters was now under fire from one camp of trotting men. They wanted to cease infusion of Thoroughbred blood into the Standardbred (trotting and pacing) breed. Historian Ken McCarr suggested that this might have been no more than a retaliatory response from fanciers of the trotter, who resented the prejudice that Thoroughbred breeders directed against their horses. People argued back and forth bitterly about breeding trotting types to Thoroughbreds. Herr took his stand. He insisted on breeding Thoroughbreds to Standardbreds, and in the end he was proved right. According to McCarr, these early Thoroughbred crosses in the bloodlines boosted the Kentucky trotters to a peerless status—the best in the United States.[18]

William Singerly, like his brother George, also loved to drive trotters for recreation. While it is unclear which brother was the first to take up the sport, both became intensely involved. Only the wealthy could afford to participate at the level the Singerly brothers played. Men such as William and George joined private driving clubs and purchased fast trotting racers that they immediately retired and hitched to their personal wheeled conveyances. In Philadelphia, the brothers served on the board of directors of the country's prestigious organization of amateurs, the Belmont Driving Club. The club had opened in 1876 in then "suburban" Philadelphia, on a road called Meeting House Lane.[19] Here aficionados tooled around the club's private track and sometimes took their fast horses onto public roads.

It was the same in Cleveland, New York, Boston, and all the northern metropolises, where post–Civil War industrialists, stock traders, and capitalists had enormous amounts of discretionary money to spend on this recreational sport. Every Sunday in New York, wealthy men drove their elegant trotters down Third Avenue and later along a speedway in Harlem, mostly to show off, although an impromptu race against another man's horse never was out of the question. *New York Ledger* owner Robert Bonner and Cornelius Vanderbilt, a tycoon among American businessmen, developed a tremendous rivalry on the roads. William C. Whitney and August Belmont also drove.[20]

One May Day in Philadelphia in 1889, members of the Belmont Driving Club arrived to great fanfare for their annual meeting, at which they elected officers. Arrivals commenced at 3:00 p.m. and continued throughout the afternoon. Each time a horse and rig pulled through the gates, members seated on the porch of the clubhouse let loose a round of great cheers. The more dust a horse raised upon its arrival the better. Newspapers made note of these fiery, snorting, whirlwind passes through the clubhouse gates: "Dan Strauss made the wind whistle as he jumped the gravel with his brown gelding Hiram Miller, closely followed by Frank Bower with the brown mare Maggie B." The club elected William president in 1885, and George frequently served as a director.[21]

William spared no amount of money when acquiring horses. Before he ventured into Thoroughbred racing, winning the Futurity at

Belmont Park in New York with Morello in 1892, Singerly concentrated on building a stable of roadsters that he took great pride in driving. His leisure time seemed solely devoted to horses and to yachting, and his taste ran to the most expensive in both. He purchased a gelding named McLeod after he won the Blue Grass Stakes at the trotting track in Lexington in 1881. William drove the gelding for four years, then turned him over to George, who rode the gelding in the saddle to a record 2:19½ over the Belmont Driving Club track. In 1898, William claimed to have lost his nerve for driving these four-footed Ferraris: "Now I am content to sit behind a coach team and let someone else do the driving." But in previous years he had blazed a comet's trail on buggy wheels and ranked among the leading amateur drivers.[22]

While George partnered in owning a Lexington farm, William more famously owned farms in Pennsylvania (Record Farm, near Gwynedd) and in Maryland (near Elkton). Some of his country guests ranked among the nation's leading men. President Cleveland, for one, discovered that he could relax at William's farms as easily as he could on the man's yachts. The yachts, like the stable of horses, consistently drew the attention of newspapers, particularly when President Cleveland was aboard. George shared his brother's fondness for yachting. When William Singerly's yacht, the *Restless*, was launched in 1887, those aboard included George and Philadelphia railroad magnate George Widener, whose family would figure prominently in Thoroughbred racing.[23]

William and George kept young racing stock in Kentucky trained exclusively by the Macey brothers in Versailles and Crit Davis in Harrodsburg. William particularly favored Davis for the man's honesty, a rare commodity among turfmen, who were viewed, quite accurately, as gamblers and speculators. William once said, "The drivers certainly would stand much better with the community and make more money by building up a reputation for integrity. Look at Budd Doble, John Murphy and Crit Davis. Wealthy men are their patrons and their stalls are always full." Following the lead of wealthy horse owners, breeders in Kentucky began to distance themselves from professional followers of the turf, including horse trainers. By the latter 1880s, Kentucky landowners and horse breeders were setting themselves above and separate from racetrack turfmen, citing the difference as "beer glass crystal" compared to "a genuine diamond."[24] Apparently, this protected the reputation of the wealthy owners as well as of Kentucky breeders. They elevated themselves in status by making a clear distinction.

Kentucky horse breeders cultivated the nuances of snobbishness, separating themselves from the men of the racecourse. They adopted this elitist stance as part of a new identity emerging in the 1890s and early 1900s that tied the Bluegrass to the plantation South of the antebellum era. This new "southern" identity replaced a "western" image that had stamped central Kentucky since the early 1800s, when the region was close to the edge of the western frontier. Not until the Gilded Age did the western image of Kentucky began to wane, a bit late, in the slipstream of a rising popularity across the nation for all things antebellum.

Perhaps people everywhere were trying to escape the present during the 1890s and early twentieth century by reverting in their imaginations to something they perceived as a more delightful age. Central Kentucky horse breeders bought into this turn of the imagination. Increasingly they saw themselves as chivalric southern gentlemen ruling ideal little estates. Members of Kentucky's landed gentry constructed the fabric of this myth in part by distancing themselves from the dishonest realm of the racecourse.

They had good reason to distance themselves, for Thoroughbred and trotting racing alike were fraught with dishonesty and corruption in the 1890s. But Kentucky breeders may have had another reason to separate themselves. The financial depression that began with the Panic of 1893 hit the horse industry hard, just at a time when Bluegrass breeders were ramping up their pitch to wealthy outsiders to invest in farmland surrounding Lexington. They needed a selling point to overcome the discouragements of this financial depression. The popular turn to a bucolic imaginary South must have seemed an idea worth promoting. And so one article read, "The word 'turf' in Kentucky brings to mind no idea of hot and dusty [betting] rings, of eager, vulgar interest, of crowds, noise and confusion; but calls up the thought of wide and cool fields, of calm and gentle breezes, of broad perfumes, and of goodly creatures' instinct with the grace and beauty of vigorous life, and fit for the scenes wherein they live."[25]

Belle's business model—gracious hospitality dispensed by a southern belle—placed her conveniently within the parameters of the rising myth. Her friendship with one or both of the Singerly brothers enabled her to play her role elegantly. Singerly money made it possible for Belle to acquire the house and furniture, expensive clothes, and polished style that recalled the Old South, or at least Old Lexington, to the men who passed through the door at 59 Megowan Street.

Had George or William been the beau of Bluegrass Belle? In the original Belle collection that Skeets Meadors compiled, he identified George as Belle's paramour and benefactor. However, Thompson noted on Meadors's typed page that this was in error. In Thompson's book, William emerges as Belle's beau. Thompson provided no written explanation for the switch.[26]

It would be a mistake to suggest that William the kingmaker never would have risked his reputation by romancing a brothel keeper. The culture of Gilded Age America tended to wink at the demimonde, whether in a metropolis or in a small city like Lexington. The Republican boss in Philadelphia, Boise Penrose, encouraged whorehouse start-ups and visited these places to offer political support. Penrose's framed photograph hung in many a house of prostitution in Philadelphia, right alongside framed photos of the sports hero of the times, prizefighter John L. Sullivan. So why would the most powerful player in Pennsylvania's Democratic Party, William Singerly, play by different rules?[27]

Belle Brezing's house was not known to display the portraits of local politicians. In that way, Lexington was more conservative than Philadelphia. But the ornate clock topped with the statue of a horse that stood prominently on the mantel in one of Belle's downstairs parlors spoke as much as any portrait could about the power structure in this small city. Money from the rising horse business making its way into Lexington was making Belle a wealthy woman. The Singerly fortune stood at the center of Belle's interests.

chapter SEVEN

Lexington's Exclusive Mansion for Men

Megowan Street had never seen commotion like Belle's opening night in 1891. All varieties of horse-drawn vehicles pulled up in front of no. 59, dropping off male passengers wearing formal evening dress. Drivers shouted to their horses. Cabs departed as quickly as they had arrived, the drivers turning their horses sharply back toward the Phoenix Hotel to pick up more fares. In the trickle-down effect the evening had on the local economy, hack drivers made a small fortune in tips on this memorable night.

Belle had invited physicians, lawyers, judges, horsemen, businessmen, and bankers to this fete. Sweet orchestral strains poured into the street every time the door opened to admit another caller. She had hired musicians for her opening, foregoing her mechanical nickelodeon. Her staff had prepared an elegant buffet. Her bar served the finest wines and champagne.

Reminiscences of Belle's grand opening lingered a long time in the world of the demimonde. These accounts never found their way into the written histories of horse country, yet tales about this party were passed from fathers to sons with a wink and a secret smile. Finally, some seventy years after the event, the evidence proving this party had really taken place emerged in the form of a photograph. A local historian, William Henry Townsend, got a close look at the photo while on a professional visit to Belle's house.[1]

Townsend went to the house in the company of Thomas D. Clark, then chairman of the history department at the University of Kentucky. These two, along with Charles Staples and J. Winston Coleman Jr., were founding members of a group of book collectors who called themselves the Book Thieves. Clark was at home one August day in 1933 when Townsend pulled into his driveway, honking his horn. Townsend yelled out the window of his car and "in a voice clear enough for all my neighbors to hear, asked me if I would like to go to a whorehouse," Clark recalled. Belle's physician, Dr. Charles A. Nevitt, had contacted Townsend and said that Belle wanted someone from the university to go through her library because she was interested in donating her books.[2]

Townsend and Clark hurried to Megowan Street. But the visit with Belle did not come about " because the old lady had suffered another sinking spell and we saw neither her nor her library," Clark wrote. On a later day, Townsend and Clark, in the company of Coleman, returned. Clark did not believe any of the books they saw were noteworthy. However, Townsend did find something very significant—a photo of the long-rumored party that Belle had inscribed, "My Opening Night, 1891." Townsend also described separate group photographs of prostitutes and their madams who had come from Memphis, Nashville, St. Louis, Louisville, and Cincinnati to attend the opening party. He found photos of Belle from various phases of her life. Most interestingly, he discovered a ledger book that he "impounded" when Belle was not looking.[3]

The photograph of Belle's opening night showed a banquet table extending the length of three parlors opened wide. On the table Townsend saw "exquisite linens, gleaming silverware, dazzling cut glass, fragile china, tall vases of American Beauty roses, [and] an orchestra behind potted palms in a far corner. At the table sat beautiful young women, appropriately costumed for such an auspicious occasion, and, incredible as it seems today, doctors, lawyers, businessmen, civic and social leaders of the city—quite a number of whom I had known . . . all immaculately clad in full dress suits, making no effort whatever to conceal their identity."[4]

Belle had seen to the remodeling of her house from the time she had acquired the building in May 1890. J. B. Moore, then a resident of East High Street, said he measured for drapes and curtains at Belle's when he worked for C. F. Brower & Co. (he called it Brower & Hicks), the former Brower & Scott where Belle had purchased her carpets in 1881 for 163 North Upper Street. Belle must have spent a fortune on furnishings, and she certainly had sufficient funds now to do so. Photographs of the interior of her house reveal elaborate draperies, plush furniture, stained glass windows, tall mirrors, and expensive carpets. The floors were exquisite, a "parquet of Honduran mahogany, native walnut, and light maple," Belle's biographer, Thompson, described. "The turned wood on the staircase, like the doors and facings throughout the house, was of rich walnut or cherry." Mirrors reflected the glow from chandeliers lighted with gas jets and, on alternate arms, the new electricity, still a novelty in Lexington. "Furniture and decoration would be the latest," Thompson wrote, "offering comfort to compare with the best men's clubs in the country." Among the furniture were chairs made from Texas Longhorn steers, given to Belle by an admirer.[5]

The house stood two and a half stories tall. It stood much taller in Belle's pride, considering how far in life she had come. Now thirty-one, she had scaled the strata of her shadow world from prostitute to wealthy madam with friends in high places. She held a powerful position as confidante to men of great importance in business, society, and government. Singerly was one example of her well-placed friends. Another was a police judge, John J. Riley, whose offices and residence were at 229 West Short Street.

Riley dealt lightly and sympathetically with prostitutes brought into police court. Thompson told a story about Judge Riley's treatment of prostitutes rounded up in a police dragnet shortly before the elections of 1897. He asked the occupation of each, and individually they all responded, "Dressmaker." He asked the same of a woman he knew quite well standing near the end of the line.

"Judge, you know I'm a whore," she responded.

The unflappable Judge Riley replied, "How's business?"

The prostitute said, "Lousy as hell, Judge, with all these dressmakers around."[6]

Eventually, Riley fell in love with a prostitute working at Belle's place. He left the bench, and the two moved into a residence at 145 Deweese Street. Clara Sayre recalled he was "crazy about the girl," and later they married, moving to a better part of town. Judge Riley was not the only one to marry a girl working at Belle's place, according to

Sayre. Several women married men they met at the house. "Mostly they were men who lived away from here and had come here for the running races or the trots," Sayre said. "They would take their new wives back to wherever they lived and nobody there would know about the girls' past." But, she added, "Everybody in Lexington knew where Judge Riley got his wife."[7]

Belle's hope for avoiding harassment seemed to rest on a more secure foundation in her new neighborhood. City authorities, and most especially the police, appeared to allow the presence of prostitution on Megowan Street, unlike on North Upper Street. Megowan and a few surrounding streets were in the early stages of turning into a red-light district. As such, they were part of a late-nineteenth-century phenomenon arising in numerous American cities. Red-light districts represented the cutting edge of social thought. These districts were in practice informally legalized prostitution. As long as brothels remained restricted to certain neighborhoods, the police generally left them alone. Good and decent citizens were not openly accepting prostitution—they were simply pushing it out of sight. Victorian Americans had decided that segregated prostitutes would be unable to pollute the morals of the community.[8]

At least seventy-six American cities had red-light districts during the later 1890s. Among these were the Barbary Coast in San Francisco, Storyville in New Orleans, the Levee in Chicago, and the Tenderloin in New York. A police chief in Chicago guaranteed red-light district denizens complete freedom from interference. In a written notice, he promised that persons "involved in prostitution who confined their business to the west of Wabash Avenue and to the east of Wentworth Avenue would remain immune from police harassment."[9]

Segregation of prostitutes occurred at the same time that white Americans were segregating society along racial lines. Not by chance did red-light districts in Lexington and Louisville, for example, end up in African American neighborhoods.[10] Officials didn't ask residents of these neighborhoods if they wanted prostitutes to move in, because black voices did not count. A letter written to Kentucky governor Simon Buckner seeking a pardon for brothel keeper Sue Green made an argument that any white person of the time would have understood. The charge against Green had no validity, the letter stated, because the complainants were "negroes in small frame houses" living in the designated red-light district. As the writer of this letter pointed out, various grand juries had refused to indict prostitutes on Megowan Street "on the ground that in a city of the size of Lexington such houses will of necessity exist and this house both as to character and location is less objectionable than it could possibly be at any other place."[11]

In Lexington, people began to refer to the red-light district as "the Hill" because Megowan Street ran uphill from Main Street. The climb required a bit of effort on the part of hack horses and men making the journey on foot. Most would have said the effort was worth it. "The Hill" became shorthand for a shadow world that good folk in Lexington claimed to know nothing about—despite the fact that many good folk knew their way up that hill quite well. In truth, the red-light district operated very much in synergy with the city. Brothel operators required grocery deliveries. Their "girls" required clothing. Wine merchants and beer distributors enjoyed a lucrative business with these houses of ill fame. Bourbon distillers also made money off Belle's business. Kentuckians had been manufacturing bourbon since early in the nineteenth century, and they held this unique whiskey in equal regard with their racehorses. Commerce and business functioned in synchrony with the Hill, even if Lexington confined the Hill to the shadows.

Belle wanted no trouble from the police or courts. Protectors such as Judge Riley likely had assured her that prostitution could operate freely on Megowan Street. Nonetheless, she turned away the type of customers who might bring problems to her door. Belle screened her clientele by charging high fees. In the parlance of the Hill, Belle's place was a $5 house surrounded by $2 houses. She also made every effort to ensure that selling alcohol to her clients would not bring trouble, purchasing a retail liquor license from the Internal Revenue Service.[12]

Belle had set the bar for houses of ill fame in this small city, and her influence extended beyond Kentucky. Two women from Kentucky known infamously as the Everleigh sisters showed Belle's influence in the brothel they opened in Chicago. Minnie and Ada Everleigh opened the doors of their resort for men in 1904. They favored Belle's lavish style but took their interior design much farther. They saw to the construction of nearly soundproof rooms. They gave each parlor a different name: the Moorish Room, the Music Room, the Japanese Room, the

Egyptian Room, and the more prosaically named Rose, Green, and Blue rooms. The sisters designed the Copper, Silver, and Gold rooms for the mining kings whose fortunes would have rendered them highly sought after as clients.[13]

Opening night at the Everleigh sisters' house was a lot like Belle's opening night, with champagne, wine, and two string quartets playing. The Everleighs had brought a bit of the South with them to Chicago; their success prompted competitors to adopt southern touches. One brothel replaced its white help with black servants, served southern dishes at its buffet, and informed the resident prostitutes they would now act like ladies. The prostitutes learned they would wear evening gowns instead of their brief attire. They were to receive daily instruction in etiquette. Everyone, everywhere, wanted a taste of the antebellum South, precisely the formula Belle had served up with remarkable success.[14]

Like Belle, the Everleigh sisters did not suffer clients with thin wallets. Clients frequently spent $1,000 in a single evening at this Chicago brothel; the minimum expense appeared to be $100. Admittance required a letter of recommendation, a proper introduction, or at the very least an engraved card. Like Belle, the sisters did not tolerate rowdy behavior. Among the thirty or so women who may have worked at any one time at this house was a former New York socialite—or so claimed her husband, William Earle Dodge Stokes, after Rita Hernandez de Aba de Acosta Stokes sued him for divorce.[15]

The Stokes couple had cut quite a swath through Lexington after purchasing a farm that they named in honor of their horse, Patchen Wilkes. Stokes, heir to a fortune of $11 million, married Rita in 1895 when she was nineteen years old—and fifteen years his junior. Her family had emigrated from Cuba. Stokes fell in love with Rita after seeing her picture displayed in the window of a Fifth Avenue photographer's studio. Someone had pronounced her "the most nearly perfectly beautiful woman in the world." Stokes gave her the Kentucky farm and a famous horse named Beuzetta, a trotter and winner of the Kentucky Futurity, for which he paid $16,000.[16] Five years later, during divorce proceedings, Stokes would accuse Rita of working at the Everleigh sisters' house. But early in their marriage, upon acquiring their horse farm, the Stokeses kept Bluegrass Kentuckians agog for other reasons. They were eccentric and profligately displayed their tremendous wealth.

They entertained out-of-town guests with southern parody at Patchen Wilkes, throwing their "Negro Ball," intended to express the "southern" qualities of the lifestyle the Stokeses adopted whenever they visited their Kentucky farm. The ball was lavish: workers decorated the interior of a brick horse barn with bunting and flags and laid down a canvas dance floor covering over half the floor of the barn. Occupying the other half was a large table, said to be 110 feet long. Caterers spread out fruit and large cakes on the table and served "a supper such as negroes would enjoy," the *New York Times* reported. The stereotypical menu featured roast shoat and sweet potatoes, fried fish and coffee, fruits, pickles, ice cream, and cake.[17]

Rita Stokes sent out two hundred invitations to African Americans. The *New York Times*'s headline revealed the exotic appeal the Negro Ball held for her and the friends she invited from New York: "Mrs. Stokes's Negro Ball: How the New York Woman Entertains the Colored People on Her Kentucky Farm." The implication was that Rita Stokes slipped into the role of a southern belle when she and her traveling circus of ogling acquaintances stepped off the train in the Bluegrass. The invited African Americans quite helpfully supplied the appropriate exotic entertainment, engaging in "buck dances" and the "cakewalk." The evening was all very minstrelsy, all very Jim Crow, and all so very *southern*. "Southern" was the image Belle had perfected many years earlier at her mansion for men.

Belle may have watched the races in close proximity to Rita Stokes at the trotting track. Rita owned a stable of fast trotters and pacers that raced in Lexington during the annual October meet. In 1896, a pair of her horses, Miss Rita and Josie B., set a world's double team record at the trotting track. Her husband similarly took a great interest in trotters. With considerable assistance from his farm manager, Peter Duryea of New York, he developed Patchen Wilkes Farm into one of the major trotting horse nurseries in the Bluegrass.[18]

Outsiders like the Stokeses were beginning to liven up central Kentucky with the self-indulgent lifestyles their immense wealth afforded them. The locals must have regarded all this with a sense of awe, for outsiders still remained a novelty in Lexington and would into the early 1900s. The landed estates of Bluegrass Kentucky shown in a map of 1887 reveal breeding farms owned and operated largely by resident owners. It was not yet apparent that the region stood on the cusp of an influx of absentee landowners who would bring immense fortunes into horse country.

As nostalgia for the antebellum South became increasingly popular into the early 1900s, these wealthy outsiders understood they were buying lifestyle as well as land. They might visit their farms only once or twice a year, but while in residence, they saw themselves as country squires overseeing their bucolic domains. This escape was most appealing, given that labor strikes, immigration, servant problems, and a long list of woes troubled their urban lifestyles back home. Lexington and central Kentucky, stuck in the past, held nostalgic appeal that became increasingly popular with those who could afford to buy the land and the way of life that came with it: a well-ordered existence where "the darkies are trained as perfectly as the horses. Everything has its place, and everything in its place, would seem to be the order of the day."[19] No one was getting out of line here. Not even the prostitutes in their restricted district.

Milton Sanford, a textiles magnate from the Northeast, had stood alone in the 1870s as an outsider owning a Bluegrass horse farm: the Preakness Stud, which Dan Swigert later purchased and renamed Elmendorf. Outside money did not begin pouring into the Bluegrass until August Belmont, the New York financier and society leader, moved his breeding operation, Nursery Stud, from Long Island to Lexington in 1885.

In 1892, Lamon Harkness purchased Walnut Hall Farm. An Ohioan, he was a son of S. V. Harkness, one of the founders of the Standard Oil Company. The Bluegrass locals at first assumed he was a rich man playing with his millions, but he soon proved them wrong. When it came to trotters, Lamon Harkness knew the horse business as well as he knew the oil business.[20]

James Ben Ali Haggin acquired Elmendorf in 1902. James R. Keene purchased Castleton Farm in 1903. These outsiders were absentee landowners who visited only occasionally. But the big money they brought into the Bluegrass enabled the horse business to expand, thereby expanding the local economy. Belle Brezing profited from this expansion: her business grew parallel to the horse business. Her name was soon known in faraway places such as Argentina, as some Kentuckians discovered while delivering horses to South America.

Within Lexington's red-light district, no. 59 Megowan stood in a class by itself. Blanche Patterson, one of Belle's prostitutes who eventually opened a house of her own on Megowan Street, operated the next-best house. Blanche went to work for Belle as a prostitute after losing her job at the Bogaert jewelry store. She told how Belle provided her new girls with nice clothing, charging them on an installment plan until they had repaid the cost. Blanche said Belle charged her girls $24 weekly for laundry, room and board, maid service, and towels. The girls kept the rest of the money they earned at Belle's rate of $5 per client. They also kept their tips. These sometimes amounted to $10, although during the trotting races (and presumably the Thoroughbred races as well), the tips frequently ran higher. Blanche related that during the trots it was nothing for a trotting horseman sitting in the parlor, hoping for luck at the next day's races, to slip a $50 bill into a girl's stocking.[21]

"Miss Belle never insisted that a girl drink with the customer if that girl didn't drink," Blanche recalled. "But she sure had better order a drink if a man offered to buy." Beer sold for 5¢ a bottle at most places; Belle charged $1 a bottle and $5 for a bottle of wine. Blanche recalled that Belle had positioned large brass cuspidors all around the parlors so that her girls could empty their drinks in these if they chose.[22]

Belle had strict rules of decorum. She did not permit her girls to sit outside on the porch or beckon to prospective clients from the windows. When the girls stepped out downtown, Belle required that they dress modestly and behave properly. She told them they must never show that they recognized a customer if they saw him off the premises.

Clara Sayre moved from Cincinnati to take a job with Belle. She was just sixteen when a peddler came to her house. No one else was home. Clara admired the contents of his pack: laces, shawls, and other bits of finery. The peddler in turn complimented her beauty. He asked how she would like to work in Belle Brezing's famous house in Lexington, telling her how much money she could make. The peddler made it sound so attractive that Clara told him she would like it. A few days later, she received a telegram from Belle that said, "Come at once." Belle wired her a train ticket. The peddler probably received a procurement commission.[23]

Sayre was not her original surname; she adopted it after falling in love with Ephraim Sayre Jr., one of Belle's best customers. Clara continued to live at Belle's after Sayre became her beau, although only as a boarder; she no longer worked as a prostitute. Sayre paid Clara's $24 weekly board, dressed her in beautiful clothes, and took her on outings about town, including to the Opera House. But Eph Sayre Jr. died young, at age thirty-seven, forcing Clara to return to work in Belle's house. Not for long, however. Soon Clara met another man at Belle's who wanted her to be his exclusively. This was Clem Beachey Jr., one of the most colorful trotting horsemen to race in Lexington. He purchased a house not far from Belle's on Curley Avenue (then called East Short Street Extended), where he installed Clara.[24]

Beachey had come to Lexington in the early 1890s, bringing with him four trotting colts belonging to his father, Clem Beachey Sr., of Lebanon, Ohio. Beachey Sr. had been in the trotting business since 1866, preparing trotters for the track and the road while also operating a livery stable.[25] He instructed Beachey Jr. in the ways of these intricately gaited horses. Eventually, the son surpassed his father, becoming a successful driver at the highest level of the sport, the Grand Circuit. Like his father, Beachey Jr. was congenial and popular. Among his major clients during the early 1900s was a woman, Miss Katherine L. Wilkes, an oddity during an era when few women owned racing stables. Wilkes bred trotters at her Cruickston Park at Galt, Ontario, and sent a sizeable number—twelve in 1911—to Beachey Jr.'s Lexington-based training stable. Sometimes Wilkes sent her superintendent, James Weatherill, to Lexington with the horses. Occasionally she attended races in the city.[26]

Beachey Jr. used the house on Curley Avenue for entertaining his patrons during the race meets. Clara served as hostess. "Clem never lost a dime keeping this place up the year around," Clara once said. "He could get it all back, and lots more, too, during the trots." Beachey's practice was to take his visiting clients around to inspect unraced yearlings at a variety of farms during the mornings. The clients attended the trots during the afternoons. In the evenings, Beachey invited them to his little house, where Clara poured drinks, dispensed hospitality, and just happened to know where they could find female companionship nearby.[27]

As Clara poured the liquor, Beachey would wait for the right time to make his pitch on a horse he was trying to sell. He might say something like, "You know that bay colt we were looking at this morning at Ernest Featherstone's? He looks just what we need for the two-year-old stakes next year. I can buy him for you for $15,000." Beachey, the personable and hospitable host, usually got that $15,000 or whatever amount he was asking for a horse. He would make his money from commissions on the sale of these horses. Or he might have prepurchased the colt for an option of, perhaps, $5,000, thus pocketing the extra $10,000. Clara once said, "I have known him to sell $100,000 worth of horses right here in this house during a Trots meeting."[28]

And what of Ernest Featherstone? He would be holding forth nearby at Belle's place, making his horse deals from the comfort of the mansion's clubby parlors. Belle's house was open to Featherstone for all his entertainment needs. These entertainments usually involved selling horses, but not always. Featherstone and his friends frequently organized dove shoots, an autumn sport long popular among Kentuckians. At the end of the day, they would bring the birds they had shot to Belle's to be dressed and cooked. Belle's kitchen staff would pluck the doves and prepare them for dinner, set for an hour when the happy hunters returned for what was always an outstanding meal.[29]

During the 1890s, Elias J. "Lucky" Baldwin would have been just the sort of sporting man to visit Belle Brezing's. And, since according to Clara Sayre, Belle patronized the races at Churchill Downs, she might also have come in contact with him there. After all, the Californian raced his horses in Kentucky and periodically visited the state's Thoroughbred tracks. Baldwin loved fast horses and young women. At fifty-six, he married for the fourth time, taking a sixteen-year-old to the altar. Baldwin installed his new wife in a mansion in San Francisco while he kept steady company with various mistresses. This did not go well for Baldwin—two women shot him at different times. Another, who was a mere fifteen years old, sued him for breach of promise when he was fifty-nine. Another sued him for "seduction," but Baldwin denied that charge. His reason: the woman was thirty-one and therefore too old. "Anyone who has seen her would not credit her charge against me," he said.[30]

Baldwin's stable of horses ranked among the most successful in the United States. His Thoroughbreds included Mollie McCarthy, which lost for the first time ever after Baldwin shipped her to Louisville to race against the mighty Bluegrass horse Ten Broeck. He owned the champion Emperor of Norfolk and Volante, which won the American Derby. (Volante, celebrated winner of thirty-three races, wound up in Lexington—pulling a dirt cart on the streets after the horse's usefulness on the track had ended.) Baldwin signed the great jockey Isaac Murphy to a $10,000 annual retainer. He also developed the town of Arcadia, California, which became the site of Santa Anita Racetrack. He had come far since moving to California as a young man of twenty-five in 1853. He wealth came largely from mining stock worth at least $15 million. According to rumor, he carried with him a tin box containing $1 million in pocket change.[31]

Whenever Baldwin shipped his racehorses east, he sent with them on the train his English four-in-hand coach and silver-plated harness. At Louisville, he drove the coach up to the Galt House and asked for a suite of rooms. The hotel manager was aghast. The problem was not Baldwin or his showy English coach. The jaw-dropper was the bevy of young women loaded into the coach. The women were popping out of the windows and doors, putting on quite a show. The manager told Baldwin this just would not do; the Galt House had standards. Baldwin's response was to draw attention to the pearl-handled pistol strapped to his hip. Then he pulled a roll of $1,000 bills from his pocket and waved it in front of the manager. He got his suite of rooms. On subsequent visits he always stayed at the Galt House.[32]

Belle had been in her house not quite five years when, late on the morning of March 16, 1895, a fire broke out. She was in New York at the time, possibly shopping for the latest New York fashions. The fire started in Belle's apartment, soon spreading through the upper portion of the house. Some blocks away, at the Central Fire Station on Short Street, the alarm sounded and great commotion commenced. The horses sprang from their open stalls on hearing the bell and moved into their customary positions in front of each wagon. At the jerk of a rope, the horses' harnesses fell from a ceiling apparatus onto their backs. The firemen tightened the harness in place and, with drivers up, sent the horses flying off to the fire. First away from the western doorway was the chemical wagon with its one-hundred-gallon water tank, forty-two pounds of soda, and forty-two pounds of acid. When mixed at the fire, these chemicals were designed to extinguish or at least slow the fire even before a hose truck arrived and hooked up to a water hydrant.[33]

Fire wagons proceeding to a fire made considerable noise, the firemen sounding gongs along the route by pushing pedals with their feet. "Here they come like a storm," read one contemporary description of the rush to reach a fire. "The driver stooping down with slacked rein, speaking to the intent steeds that, big-eyed, wide-nostriled and strained, go thundering on. . . . Look out! They pass a crossing like an earthquake on wheels. The horses, alive and stung with the same enthusiasm which filled the firemen, spurn the rough street, and dash along as if a prairie on fire was chasing them. They need no whip, they need no lash, their big arteries are churning with hot blood; their big muscles are strung to the task they love. The wild horse, followed fast by red fire, never sped like they. With ears laid back, with eyes standing out from the bony face, with nostrils red as blood, they gallop on untiring."[34]

In Lexington, a fire engine dog named Nice always ran ahead of the engines. His job was to bark a warning to anyone who might be standing in the way of the charging horses. Nice came to his job naturally; he had chased fires for a long time before he joined the company. Firemen noticed that he ran on his own accord to every fire. The chief decided to adopt the dog and appoint him to a professional position. The firemen originally named the dog Tramp, but soon changed his name to Nice once they realized he had dainty habits. Nice became a huge favorite among the firefighters.[35]

As the fire spread at Belle's house, about fifteen or twenty women ran outside, all of them scantily dressed in nightwear. They had been sleeping, as their days tended to begin late. One prostitute, Flora Johnston, was trapped at a window of the uppermost part of the two-and-a-half-story house. She was screaming for help. A quick-thinking onlooker ran inside the house, grabbed a mattress, and placed it outside under the window, urging Johnston to jump. J. B. Moore helped hold the mattress. The woman did jump but suffered injuries to her back.[36]

By the time the firemen arrived, smoke was rolling out of all the windows. After about an hour, the firefighters managed to extinguish the flames, but they could not save the upper portion of the house. Moreover, water damage ruined the furniture, walls, and carpets in the lower portion. The *Lexington Press-Transcript* summed up the loss succinctly, deftly naming this house for what it was without actually saying so: "The house was considered the finest in the South and the loss has not as yet been estimated."[37] The house was not the finest mansion in the South; it was the finest whorehouse. Readers understood.

Belle received a telegram in New York informing her of the fire. While she was on her way back to Lexington, the townspeople raved about the bravery of firefighter Tim Maher. He had seized a ladder and entered an upper-level room to retrieve a costly set of diamonds after someone yelled out that the jewelry would be lost. Maher charged into the room amid billowing smoke and rescued the diamonds. Nearly all else in the house was lost.[38]

But Belle carried an insurance policy worth about $40,000, and she decided to rebuild. With this second remodeling of the house, Belle added a full third floor. She had the house painted white, possibly because the new brick did not match the old. The fire barely caused her to slacken stride at all. Regardless of what some in the community may have thought of her or of 59 Megowan, Belle was more popular than ever.

Meanwhile, brothers George and William Singerly continued their periodic visits to Lexington. According to his custom, one of these Singerlys would check into the Phoenix Hotel and send flowers to Belle's house to announce his arrival in town. When the flowers were delivered, Billy Mabon, commonly believed to be Belle's lover, knew what came next. His standing agreement with Belle was that he would move out of her house for as long as one or the other Singerly remained in town. Belle did not intend to challenge the Singerly ego with Mabon's presence in the house. Mabon appears to have accepted this arrangement. The Singerlys, after all, possessed the fortune that enabled Belle's operation.

At all other times, Mabon lived with Belle in her private apartment in the house. One photo shows him seated comfortably in the sitting room, thoroughly at home. But Mabon always maintained his own quarters at various places in Lexington. He clearly loved Belle. Pink Thomas recalled that when Belle returned home from one of her trips out of town and Mabon saw her traveling trunks unloaded at the house, he would come down to the street to meet her as she alighted from the cab. "He had her room all fixed up with flowers and everything,"

Thomas said. "And he hugged and kissed her and just patted her. He couldn't have treated her better if she had been a queen."[39]

One night when one of the Singerly brothers was in the house, two men from prominent local families got into a fight. Customarily, Belle's bouncer—a former sparring partner for two heavyweight champions, Jim Corbett and Bob Fitzsimmons—would have thrown the rowdy ones out of the house. But Singerly stopped her. He told Belle, "Let them go at it. I'll pay for any damage they do." The men broke up furniture, pictures, mirrors, and bric-a-brac. Their fight moved all over the house, on all three floors and on the staircases between floors. Eventually they wore themselves out. They had another drink, departed the house together, and were heard singing as they walked down the hill to Main Street. The next morning, Singerly presented Belle with a check for $10,000, saying he had never had a more enjoyable evening.[40] Did he think this was how the other half lived?

As for Mabon, he suffered various small humiliations in addition to the large one. For example, the very bed Mabon slept in at Belle's may have been given to her by still another of her admirers.[41] This was Charles "Riley" Grannan, a notorious gambler whose fame spread throughout the United States and Europe. Riley Grannan gambled constantly. Ordinary people of the 1890s would read about the big "plungers" like Grannan and marvel at their highs and lows. They would lose fortunes in a single bet, then remake these fortunes on another horse race. Grannan's exploits placed him on a playing field with those high rollers who frequented Saratoga: "Pittsburg Phil" Smith, Mike Dwyer, and "Diamond" Jim Brady. Brady's girlfriend was the actress Lillian Russell. Grannan enjoyed the companionship of Miss Belle.

Grannan was born into a working-class family in Paris, Kentucky, perhaps in the late 1860s. He entered the world of work in the 1870s. From Paris he went to Cincinnati and then down to New Orleans. In both cities, he worked in hotels where he came in contact with gamblers and bookmakers. Grannan had not grown up gambling. But in New Orleans he drew the interest of first one bookmaker, then another, who saw traits in Grannan they considered worth cultivating. Grannan observed closely for two or three years as he assembled the capital needed to go out on his own. People noticed that Grannan seemed to have no idea of the value of money when he made his wagers. Grannan bet money "like [it was] tissue paper when he had it, and when he lost it did not sit down and whimper, but began looking about for some way to get it back," the *Live Stock Record* reported from its headquarters in Lexington. "Last fall, when he left Nashville for San Francisco, he lost heavily, and it was currently reported that he had but $15,000 left. He had not been in California more than three months when he won $97,000."[42]

Grannan's most memorable winning bet was on a horse named Henry of Navarre, a product of New Jersey purchased by a Lexington man, Byron McClelland. Henry of Navarre's new owner brought him down by train to Lexington, where the horse made his first two career starts at the Kentucky Association track, winning one and losing the other. Henry of Navarre developed into a useful horse that season, but his finest moments would come a year later, at age three, when he won the Belmont Stakes and other big races. The horse had won nine consecutive races when the public began clamoring for him to face an earlier foe, Domino, in a rematch. The Gravesend track in New York offered $5,000 for this highly anticipated showdown. It ended in a dead heat, which meant the owners of both horses split the purse, and those who had bet on either horse collected on their wagers. Grannan must have bet every dollar he had on Henry of Navarre, reportedly $100,000, for he won so much money that he purchased a café in Lexington. He opened the Navarre Café in 1894.[43]

The café opened in a two-story brick residence on Main Street, slightly west of Walnut Street. A bridge over Main Street connected the café to the former Main Street Christian Church. At this church, in 1894, the city held an exposition to showcase Bluegrass manufacturing and other products. Grannan purchased the bed at the exposition and presented it to Miss Belle, according to one contemporary's recollections.[44]

Grannan did not remain long in the restaurant business. Nine months after he opened the café, he sold out to his partner, James H. Applegate, a well-known Lexington bookmaker, and a caterer, S. R. "Dad" Brooks. Grannan had hit one of his low places. Before he could depart for Saratoga, he received notice of two lawsuits filed against him: one for $561.75 in unpaid liquor charges and another for a painting bill of $70.20. "Grannan admitted that he was a heavy loser on the races recently," read one report, "but claimed to have property worth four times over his debts." Grannan died broke in Nevada in 1908, where a former Methodist minister, once tried and acquitted for heresy, conducted his funeral service—in a saloon.[45]

Happily, no one had to repossess Belle's bed to pay off Grannan's debts. Belle continued to sleep in the bed until close to her death thirty-two years later. But with Grannan gone, her friends were beginning to disappear.

chapter **EIGHT**

A Uniquely Powerful Woman in a Changing City

Belle's business was thriving at her whorehouse bought with Singerly money. Meanwhile, the Singerly brothers had grown restless in another phase of their sporting life. No longer content with owning only trotters, they followed a popular trend among wealthy men and got into Thoroughbred racing. William won the nation's premier horse race at that time, the Futurity, run at Coney Island in New York. But the wake of scandals that trailed William and George through Thoroughbred racing reflected the very reasons why the sport needed reform.

Thoroughbred racing in the United States had reached the highest popularity in its history during the Gay Nineties. The reasons were many. Ordinary folk had more time for leisure, and many were choosing to spend this time at Thoroughbred racecourses. Rising attendance brought in more bookmakers to handle the increased betting. Racecourses realized huge profits licensing these on-track bookmakers, the only form of wagering then in use at tracks. The tracks turned a portion of their profits into richer purses for their marquee races. This in turn drew more people to the sport.

Racing was prospering. But this prosperity revealed a darker side: a criminal element drawn to the sport to make big money. Rumors flew at the tracks of fixed races, doped-up horses, and all sorts of betting coups. The wealthiest men participating in New York racing hoped to hold off social reformers and legislators when in 1894 they organized a governing body they called the Jockey Club. It took over the licensing of jockeys and all others participating at New York tracks. The Jockey Club centralized authority. Unfortunately, it came into existence two years too late to deal with the scandal revealed after William Singerly won the Futurity with a long shot named Morello.

Morello does not stand out in the annals of Thoroughbred racing as a memorable horse. His only remarkable moment occurred when he won the 1892 Futurity. After that, the horse slipped into obscurity. Singerly also was obscure in Thoroughbred racing when on the morning of this Futurity, he assembled two hundred friends in Philadelphia for a train ride to see Morello race in New York. After the horse won, Singerly and his friends did not linger in New York for celebrations or interviews. They returned immediately to Philadelphia.[1]

A rather provincial New York press was scrambling to figure out who Singerly was—a newspaper publisher in Philadelphia, you say? Moreover, the press failed to understand why Singerly had not been listed in the program as Morello's owner. A most interesting story of duplicity began to unravel. Morello raced in the name of Frank Van Ness. Yet it appears from news accounts that people were aware that Morello's owner was in fact Singerly. The *New York Times* commenced an investigation and discovered that Singerly was not listed as owner because he was ineligible to race at Coney Island. The track operated under the governance of a body known as the Board of Control, a precursor of the Jockey Club. The Board of Control had denied Singerly a license because his horses had raced at a track in Guttenberg, New Jersey, that was operating outside the board's control. This was how Morello had come to race in the name of Van Ness. In modern times, this practice is known as "hidden ownership, an offense punishable in all racing jurisdictions throughout the United States."[2]

Singerly's lapse of good judgment did not end with the ownership issue. Morello's trainer for the Futurity was listed as James McLaughlin. The reason was that Van Ness found himself in poor standing with the Board of Control. The board had revoked his trainer's license after an incident at Morris Park, another New York track. The most peculiar part of the story was that Singerly had chosen Van Ness to train his Thoroughbreds—when the trotting sport already had expelled the man. Van Ness was in poor standing in both sports.[3]

Born in Lockport, New York, in 1850, Van Ness was the son of a horse dealer. By 1882, he had made a reputation as an excellent driver and trainer. Van Ness moved to Kentucky, where he developed a trotter named Harry Wilkes. That horse would define this trainer's career. He raced Harry Wilkes with great success throughout the United States.[4] William Singerly had once expressed the importance of honesty and good character in his trotting horse trainers. But he failed to follow his own advice upon getting into Thoroughbred racing. Van Ness, who had crossed over into training Thoroughbreds, already had acquired a reputation in trotting racing as one of the most unscrupulous of horsemen. So the puzzle was why Singerly aligned himself with Van Ness.

There was more to the story of Morello's day in New York. Shortly before the Futurity, the horse's stable learned that the jockey it had engaged was no longer available. The jockey's contract holder had decided to exercise his option of using that rider on his horse in this same race. At the last minute, McLaughlin and presumably Van Ness were scrambling to find a rider for Morello. But all the best riders already had mounts in this seventeen-horse field. McLaughlin and Van Ness asked Isaac Murphy to ride, but Murphy's contract holder would not release him. Finally, they settled on William "Papa Bill" Hayward, who went by this nickname because he was a Methuselah of a jockey, nearly fifty years old. Born in England, Hayward had been a jockey in that country before moving to the United States to ride in 1869. He was a capable hand with a horse. Still, at his age, he was a jockey well past his prime. Winning the Futurity on Morello would bring him a shining moment in this autumn of his career.[5]

The jockey problem was resolved. But Morello's stable confronted another crisis shortly before the race was scheduled to begin. A local sheriff showed up and took possession of Morello to satisfy an outstanding judgment against Van Ness. The court judgment had resulted from an incident four years earlier, in 1888, when Van Ness had bought from someone a timing watch and had promised to pay the man $180. Van Ness never came through with the money. Now that he was listed as Morello's owner, an attachment of the horse seemed like a good recourse for the previous owner of the stopwatch.[6] Singerly must have been furious. The race was about to begin, and here was a sheriff walking off with his horse. Van Ness quickly came up with $180 and turned the money over to the sheriff. Back into the barn went Morello. But the problems did not end there.

Morello was coughing. Most trainers will not run a horse with a respiratory infection; the humane practice is to scratch him. At the very least, a cold can keep a horse from performing his best; at worst, because mucus interferes with breathing, the stress that results can cause the horse to become seriously ill. Against all common sense and humane practice, Morello's connections chose to send him into the Futurity regardless. Surprisingly, Morello's cold did not hinder him in the running. He outran a filly August Belmont II owned to win. The *New York Times* noted, "Sick though the colt was, he was running with all the speed of which he is possessed, and as if he knew what was expected of him, and that thousands of dollars [wagered] were dependent on what he did." The aging Hayward rode the race of his life to win, "as if he was some forty years younger than he is," people read the next day in the *Times.* Singerly and his two hundred friends collected some $35,000 in bets they had placed with the on-track bookmakers. Then they boarded the train for Philadelphia.[7]

But Van Ness was going to prove hugely problematic for Singerly. In the following year, racing authorities at some midwestern tracks barred Morello from racing because of the trainer. The powerful board governing tracks in the South and the Midwest (called the American Turf Congress) planned to ban Van Ness because the trotting sport had banned him. Three tracks, at St, Louis, Memphis, and Nashville, had refused to license the trainer.[8]

Van Ness was in luck. Someone persuaded the American Trotting Association to lift its ban against him. By May 1893, "one of the most sensational cases in the history of the turf was finally brought to a close," the *Chicago Daily Inter Ocean* reported. The American Trotting Association had lifted a five-year ban and reinstated Van Ness. With that, the American Turf Congress lifted its ban, and Morello was free to run. The Chicago newspaper concluded, "The decision is a popular one, as Morello is a favorite among turfites, and will be a great drawing card for any track he races over."[9]

By December, more trouble arose concerning Van Ness and Singerly. Authorities at a track in San Francisco barred further entries from Van Ness because they believed he had drugged horses from Singerly's

Belle in a formal studio portrait. (Courtesy of the Belle Brezing Photographic Collection, Special Collections and Archives, University of Kentucky, Lexington.)

Belle when she was approximately eight years old, two years after the divorce of her mother, Sarah Brezing, from her stepfather, George Brezing. This photo might have been taken during the time Sarah Brezing was married to William McMeekin. (Courtesy of the Belle Brezing Photographic Collection, Special Collections and Archives, University of Kentucky, Lexington.)

Jennie Hill operated a brothel in the Mary Todd Lincoln House, where Belle worked as a prostitute for a year and a half between 1879 and 1881. (Courtesy of the Belle Brezing Photographic Collection, Special Collections and Archives, University of Kentucky, Lexington.)

The Mary Todd Lincoln House, where Belle worked for Jennie Hill, shown in later years when there was a grocery store on the first floor. (Courtesy of the Belle Brezing Photographic Collection, Special Collections and Archives, University of Kentucky, Lexington.)

The Mary Todd Lincoln House as it appeared in 2012. (Author's collection.)

The second house where Belle operated a brothel, at 194 North Upper Street, close to Fourth Street. Belle is standing at the front gate. (Courtesy of the Belle Brezing Photographic Collection, Special Collections and Archives, University of Kentucky, Lexington.)

Belle's notorious mansion for men at no. 59 Megowan Street. The third story was added after a fire in 1895. (Courtesy of the Belle Brezing Photographic Collection, Special Collections and Archives, University of Kentucky, Lexington.)

This iconic image of Belle, c. 1890, shows her seated in her private apartment at no. 59 Megowan Street. (Courtesy of the Belle Brezing Photographic Collection, Special Collections and Archives, University of Kentucky, Lexington.)

This view of one of the adjoining parlors on the main floor of Belle's mansion at no. 59 Megowan Street shows the horn furniture given her by an admirer. E. I. "Buddy" Thompson speculated that the portrait on the summer fire screen was of Daisy May Kenney, Belle's daughter. (Courtesy of the Belle Brezing Photographic Collection, Special Collections and Archives, University of Kentucky, Lexington.)

Close-up view of one of Belle's iconic Texas longhorn chairs given her by an admirer. This photo was taken shortly after her death in 1940. (Courtesy of the *Lexington Herald-Leader*.)

Billy Mabon, one of Belle's two closest male admirers, is shown seated in Belle's private apartment at no. 59 Megowan Street. (Courtesy of the Belle Brezing Photographic Collection, Special Collections and Archives, University of Kentucky, Lexington.)

Belle's bedroom at no. 59 Megowan Street, showing the bed that gambler Riley Grannan might have purchased for Belle at the 1894 Exposition in Lexington. (Courtesy of the Belle Brezing Photographic Collection, Special Collections and Archives, University of Kentucky, Lexington.)

The main staircase to the upper floors of Belle's mansion at no. 59 Megowan Street, photographed during preparations for the auction of Belle's personal property after her death in August 1940. (Courtesy of the Belle Brezing Photographic Collection, Special Collections and Archives, University of Kentucky, Lexington.)

Secretary/bookcase where one of the Book Thieves discovered a financial accounts journal and a photo album belonging to Belle. (Courtesy of the *Lexington Herald-Leader.*)

The side entrance to Belle's brothel at no. 59 Megowan Street, c. 1940. (Courtesy of the Belle Brezing Photographic Collection, Special Collections and Archives, University of Kentucky, Lexington.)

The large crowd on the first day of the auction of Belle's personal belongings filled the street in front of her house and overflowed around the corner. The auctioneer, standing with his arm raised at the center of the porch, was Sam Downing of Lexington. (Courtesy of the Belle Brezing Photographic Collection, Special Collections and Archives, University of Kentucky, Lexington.)

Studio portrait of Belle when she might have been in her late twenties or early thirties. (Courtesy of the Belle Brezing Photographic Collection, Special Collections and Archives, University of Kentucky, Lexington.)

According to E. I. "Buddy" Thompson, Belle's first biographer, the original of this portrait of Belle stood in a gold leaf frame next to her bed at no. 59 Megowan Street. (Courtesy of the Belle Brezing Photographic Collection, Special Collections and Archives, University of Kentucky, Lexington.)

Studio portrait of Belle showing her fashionably dressed, as was her custom. (Courtesy of the Belle Brezing Photographic Collection, Special Collections and Archives, University of Kentucky, Lexington.)

The row house where Belle opened her first brothel in 1881. The address, then numbered 163 North Upper Street, is currently in the 300 block. Transylvania University has owned the building since the early 1990s and uses it as a women's locker room. (Courtesy of the Belle Brezing Photographic Collection, Special Collections and Archives, University of Kentucky, Lexington.)

This is how Belle's first brothel appeared in 2013. (Author's collection.)

Belle's scrapbook, an accounts journal, a floor plan of the second floor of her house at no. 59 Megowan Street, silver cups engraved "BB," and other personal items, among them bills, cancelled checks, and torn photographs and tintypes retrieved from Belle's trash in 1940. (Courtesy of the Belle Brezing Photographic Collection, Special Collections and Archives, University of Kentucky, Lexington.)

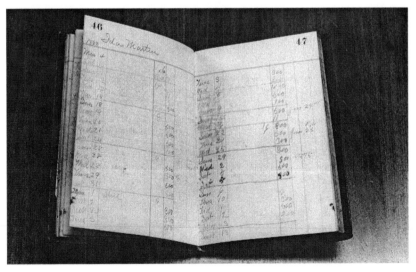

Pages in the journal in which Belle kept her accounts, 1882–1883. (Courtesy of the Belle Brezing Photographic Collection, Special Collections and Archives, University of Kentucky, Lexington.)

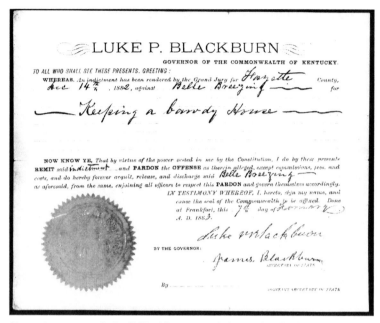

Kentucky governor Luke P. Blackburn signed this pardon for Belle on February 7, 1883, absolving her of a charge of "keeping a bawdy house." (Courtesy of the Belle Brezing Photographic Collection, Special Collections and Archives, University of Kentucky, Lexington.)

A U.S. Internal Revenue license for the retail sale of liquor issued to "Belle Breezing" on July 2, 1895, to be used at her mansion at no. 59 Megowan Street. (Author's collection.)

The family of
Belle Brearing
acknowledges with grateful
appreciation your kind expression
of sympathy

The acknowledgment of sympathy card sent as a joke by Lexington businessman Joe Graves to numerous men. (Author's collection.)

Ed Corrigan, right, winner of the 1890 Kentucky Derby with Riley. Corrigan won many races throughout the United States, frequently employing the African American riding star Isaac Murphy as his jockey. (Courtesy of the Keeneland-Cook Collection, Keeneland Library, Lexington.)

Jockey Isaac Murphy won the 1890 Kentucky Derby on Riley, owned by Ed Corrigan. Murphy at one time lived on Megowan Street, close to the house Belle purchased. Murphy also won the 1884 Kentucky Derby on Buchanan and the 1891 Kentucky Derby on Kingman. (Courtesy of the Keeneland-Hemment Collection, Keeneland Library, Lexington.)

Belle Brezing attended the races at the Kentucky Association Racecourse at Fifth and Race streets in Lexington. (Courtesy of Keeneland Library, Lexington.)

Belle's grave at Calvary Cemetery, Lexington. Her surname and year of birth are incorrect on her gravestone. (Author's collection.)

The monument Belle erected to her mother, Sarah McMeekin, on the Brezing burial plot in Calvary Cemetery. The monument is inscribed, "Blessed Are the Pure in Heart." (Author's collection.)

A fire on December 12, 1973, at the former Belle Brezing house was set by a seven-year-old boy who squirted lighter fluid over furniture in an apartment. The fire gutted several apartments and the roof and attic. (Courtesy of the *Lexington Herald-Leader*.)

View of a parlor in Belle's house taken shortly after she died in 1940. (Courtesy of the *Lexington Herald-Leader.*)

WILLIAM M. SINGERLY
The Philadelphia Record.

William Singerly, publisher of the *Philadelphia Record,* president of Belmont Driving Club, and proprietor of Elkton Stock Farm as well as an active owner of Standardbred trotters and Thoroughbred racehorses, was believed to be an admirer and financial sponsor of Belle. (Courtesy of the New York Public Library.)

Morello, winner of the Futurity, worth $40,450, run August 27, 1892, at Coney Island Jockey Club Race Course at Sheepshead Bay, New York. Morello's owner, William M. Singerly, was linked with trainer Frank Van Ness to a scandal involving the horse.

Winchester Road, c. 1910, at Hamburg Place, the Thoroughbred and Standardbred farm founded by John Madden. (*Some Roads in the Blue Grass, Constructed by Home Construction Co., Lexington, Kentucky.* Courtesy of Special Collections and Archives, University of Kentucky, Lexington.)

Harrodsburg Pike going south from Main Street, near what is now the intersection of Pyke Street. The road was (as it remains) a major thoroughfare leading into Lexington during Belle's lifetime, c. 1910. (*Some Roads in the Blue Grass, Constructed by Home Construction Co., Lexington, Kentucky.* Courtesy of Special Collections and Archives, University of Kentucky, Lexington.)

Main Street, Lexington, as Belle knew it in her youth. This image, taken before the Civil War, is looking eastward near the intersection of South Mulberry (later Limestone) Street. The Phoenix Hotel stands at the corner of Main and Mulberry streets. (Courtesy of the George Arents Collection, the New York Public Library, Astor, Lenox, and Tilden Foundations.)

Belle's scrapbook contains mostly cutouts and illustrations but also includes a few poems. (Courtesy of Special Collections and Archives, University of Kentucky, Lexington.)

Elkton Stable to induce them to run faster.[10] Any reasonable man would have fired this horse trainer by now, but Singerly stood by Van Ness.

Two years later, in 1895, Singerly's Elkton Stable came under fire once again. A jockey riding one of the Elkton horses in a steeplechase at San Francisco tried to prevent it from winning. Usually, when something like this happened, the reason was that someone had paid the jockey to throw the race. Track authorities ordered the jockey off the grounds. But once more, Frank Van Ness's name came up. Someone fingered him as the brains behind the attempt to lose the race. The *Philadelphia Inquirer* opined that Singerly's "acquaintances and friends would be delighted to see him rid himself of Van Ness and his gang."[11] Still, it appears that no one from the sporting press asked Singerly why he stubbornly stood behind Van Ness. Only Singerly knew the reason.

George Singerly was following William's lead into Thoroughbred racing. He planned to headquarter his stable in New York where, in the view of the *New York Times,* any association with Van Ness would be problematic. The *Times* speculated that the Board of Control would not license Van Ness, who had charge of George's horses. Therefore George Singerly was wasting his time setting up his stable in New York.[12]

The Singerly brothers continued to attend the trotting horse meets in Lexington, which outranked the Thoroughbred meets in popularity at this time. The Thoroughbred track had slid into financial distress. The Kentucky Association had taken on $62,500 in debt after building a new grandstand, clubhouse, and betting shed in 1889. The timing was wrong. The country would fall into a long financial depression beginning with the Panic of 1893. Unable to pay off this debt, the association dropped most of the stakes races from its autumn program. A new Kentucky Association formed to continue the racing programs at the track. But this group failed to shore up the track's finances for very long. In 1897, a mortgage on the property was foreclosed. The storied track was forced to close in 1898 after a seven-day spring meeting. The track remained shuttered for eight years, until 1905.[13]

The track had declined considerably from two decades earlier, when the greatest race ever run on this course took place on May 10, 1876. The winner of the inaugural Kentucky Derby, Aristides, faced Ten Broeck, the fastest horse of the era, at distances from one to four miles. In the officials' stand sat two former Kentucky governors, James F. Robinson and Beriah Magoffin, along with Senator James Beck and other notable Kentuckians. The racing association proudly flew a purple silk banner from the flagstaff of the judges' stand proclaiming in bright gold letters: "Kentucky Association, 1826." All recognized this as a historical reminder of the track's founding year. Aristides defeated Ten Broeck, the only other starter in the race, but the effort required Aristides to run so fast that he set an American record of 3:34½ for the two and one-eighth miles.[14]

The fate of this storied racecourse mirrored the financial free fall that most of the nation suffered after the Panic of 1893. The Panic grew out of ill-advised speculation that led to railroads overextending themselves. The powerful Philadelphia and Reading Railroad set off the spiral with its bankruptcy. More railroads failed, leading to bank failures at the many institutions holding notes on railroads. What followed was the worst financial depression the nation had seen to that time. Unemployment reached 19 percent and higher in some places.

Times grew so desperate that Jacob Coxey's ragtag procession of unemployed men marched on Washington, D.C., in an effort to get help. Coxey was a curiosity. He, his wife, and his son, named Legal Tender Coxey, rode in a carriage while the "army" of the unemployed marched behind them on foot. Coxey briefly owned a horse farm in Lexington, but that fact is almost lost to historical memory. In Washington, authorities arrested him for walking on the grass.

Like so many industries, the horse business of central Kentucky crashed during this depression. The racecourse in Lexington was only one fatality. Another was the business of Bernard J. Treacy, former city councilman from the Third Ward and co-owner of the largest stock sales and livery stable in Lexington. (Recall Treacy for the imbroglio that arose when he sold an overpriced fire horse to the city.) He also owned Ashland Park Stock Farm, a close neighbor to the Clay family's Ashland estate and stock farm at the eastern limits of Lexington. Ashland Park turned out a large number of highly successful trotting horses. Treacy also was successful as a breeder and owner of Thoroughbreds. But in the depression that followed the Panic of 1893, Treacy estimated that he lost $100,000. He said three-quarters of the horse breeders in the Bluegrass were ruined over the four years after the Panic. Those who managed to stay in the business lost fortunes. Nationwide, people dumped pedigreed horses on the markets, taking any price they could get. The value of Thoroughbred yearlings declined by 42 percent from 1894 to 1895. In many cases, horses received no bids. Their owners took huge losses.[15]

Still another horse breeder, Wickliffe Preston, suffered so many financial losses that he, too, had to sell his horses. The day of the auction, January 24, 1894, brought a diverse crowd to the Preston estate. Candidates for city offices circulated among livestock buyers. The Preston family served burgoo to the crowd. The horses sold for almost nothing. The fortunes of the Preston family had fallen far from the years before the Panic, when Wickliffe Preston had described his wheat crop as "dollar wheat."[16]

Belle's business did not suffer the precipitous declines that so many others experienced. Men kept coming to her door. When she did take time off, she went to the horse races. This meant going out of town to other tracks, since the Kentucky Association racetrack had closed. Belle was at the track in Cincinnati one day when she generously came to the aid of some tapped-out bettors from Lexington. She had gone to the races with ten gentlemen friends and her female friend Pink Thomas. They all were drinking wine. Belle planned to stay in Cincinnati overnight. She told Thomas, "If I get too drunk, call for me at the hotel tomorrow. I'm not registered as Brezing but Kenney." The next afternoon, Belle was back at the races, "looking as fresh as could be with a half [pint] in front of her and we had another drink." Some Lexington men, whom Thomas called "boys from home," stopped to say hello to Belle. She asked how they were doing, and they told her they had gone broke early in the afternoon. Belle gave them $30 and told them that if they won they could pay her back. But if they lost, they did not owe her anything.[17]

Mabon always welcomed Belle home, even if he had to leave this home whenever a Singerly showed up. But he wouldn't have to endure the Singerly presence much longer. The lingering effects of the financial depression that closed the track in Lexington also ruined William Singerly's business career. His problems centered largely on his bank in Philadelphia, the Chestnut Street National Bank. The institution's doors failed to open the morning of December 23, 1897. The bank's failure also took down the Chestnut Street Trust and Savings Fund Company, which occupied the same building and practically shared a board of directors with Singerly's bank. "The closing of the bank caused a sensation in the financial community," read a report in the *New York Herald-Tribune*. A few days later, a plan emerged to use stock in Singerly's newspaper, the *Philadelphia Record*, to aid in bailing out the bank and trust company.[18]

The bankruptcy sent Singerly on a devastating tumble over the cliff's edge. He had served as a virtual kingmaker in the Democratic Party of Pennsylvania. His influence with the national Democratic Party was similarly strong, for, as previously mentioned, he played a major role in putting Grover Cleveland in the White House. Newspapers periodically reported on Cleveland taking a few days off here and there on Singerly's yacht or at Singerly's livestock farm in Pennsylvania. Now Singerly had joined the ranks of those many Americans whose businesses had failed.

Singerly made no more visits to the Bluegrass. Two months after the bankruptcy, he was dead at age sixty-five. He had been sitting in his bedroom, smoking a cigar, when a violent coughing fit seized him. He died immediately. His physicians blamed his long-standing smoking habit, but many believed the stress of the bank failure had caused his death.[19]

George Singerly lived until 1902.[20] Belle carried on, for she certainly was capable of conducting business without one Singerly or the other. Beginning with Judge Riley, she had established and nurtured connections that placed her within a powerful circle in the Bluegrass. She operated as an equal with any man who walked through her door. She had the confidence of influential men. She held an investment portfolio. She saw huge horse deals and political deals sealed in the parlors of her house. Belle inhabited a sphere that was almost unique for a woman in Lexington during those times.

Meanwhile, other women engaged in more mundane activities, such as debating whether to remove their hats in church or whether to smoke "tea cigarettes." On the matter of hats in church there should be no debate, the *Morning Herald* informed the women of Lexington. St. Paul had spoken out against women appearing in churches with their heads uncovered. The Episcopal Church had ruled that women should cover their heads at all times in church. The invitations for a recent wedding had included a line of engraved print advising that women should not enter the church with uncovered heads.[21]

Smoking constituted a more difficult debate, but New York society had reached agreement on a new etiquette about cigarettes. Lexington women began to emulate the new mode. In New York, a countess had introduced society to "tea cigarettes," no larger than matchsticks. Any hostess could fashion these little cigarettes, substituting black tea leaves for tobacco. Hostesses were to offer the cigarettes in a white satin-lined case. The time to serve them was at 5:00 tea or after dinner, when the women and men retired to separate parlors; the men to smoke their cigars and the women their tea cigarettes. A woman might also indulge in her own home after dinner with her husband. "The pleasure of puffing a good Havana in the evening, a wife opposite with a cigarette that neither unsexes her nor impregnates her breath with tobacco, is simply irresistible," the people of Lexington read in their *Morning Herald*.[22]

These rousing debates occurred during the same month that the Women's Club devoted the first fifteen minutes of a meeting to discussion of *Quo Vadis* under the auspices of the club's Department of Literature.[23] One can imagine Belle's amusement that women would be so engaged. But then, Belle would not have been invited to attend the Women's Club.

The previous year, 1896, the Women's Club of central Kentucky had stepped onto a larger civic stage and successfully influenced change of far-reaching proportions. Mrs. Mary Dudley Short read a paper she wrote on the merits of standard time. The club invited city officials to the reading of Short's paper, in which she pointedly informed them that all major cities in the United States had operated under standard time since Sunday noon, November 18, 1883—but not Lexington. The people of the Bluegrass lived and worked according to solar time (also called sun time and even God's time) because landowners and farmers exercised a disproportionate amount of power in the region. One citizen had reaffirmed the reality of this political control in a letter to the editor of the *Kentucky Leader* in 1891:

Without wishing to disparage the hope of the idealists who wish to make Lexington a manufacturing center, we must give expression to the opinion entertained by every sound thinking person that that can never be accomplished. Central Kentucky is pre-eminently an agricultural and stock raising country, and nothing else can be made out of it. . . .

Every trial so far in that direction has been an utter failure. . . . They contributed about $25,000 to the lock factory. . . . The result was they had to sell out their patents and machinery to a Louisville company who put in $250,000 in cash, and they are doing today the largest business of the kind in the United States. . . .

It was the same way with the twine factory, though the hemp grows right here, and in that respect had the advantage over the lock factory. Now the hemp is shipped away, made into twine somewhere else, and then shipped back as twine, and used by our farmers proportionately in greater quantity than anywhere else.[24]

It was one thing to lament that Lexington might never change; it was something else to arrive in Lexington by train (or try to leave the city) and discover that the train schedules operated twenty-two minutes earlier than the time posted on Lexington clocks. Tempers raged in the debate over abandoning God's time in this bucolic Eden. But how could you modernize a city where people entered a time warp the minute they stepped off the train? Many efforts to synchronize Lexington time with the time of the outside world had failed. In 1883, the mayor had ordered the clocks changed to standard time but rescinded the order within an hour because of heated opposition. Finally, the Women's Club of central Kentucky decided that enough was enough. The time had arrived to synchronize clocks with those in the rest of the United States.[25]

The Women's Club pressed forward with its mission. The *Morning Herald* ran the full text of Short's speech. The city council voted to accept standard time. All clocks except one were turned back twenty-two minutes in March 1896. The holdout was the county courthouse clock, which remained on solar time for another three months. It took a tiebreaker vote of the Fayette County Fiscal Court to nudge the courthouse crowd into modernity, but standard time finally replaced solar time on June 5, 1896, at 12:40 p.m.[26] No excuses from this point on if you missed your train.

The city was changing in other ways, too. By 1890, electric arc lamps had replaced gas streetlights. In the same year, the first electric streetcar ran from the car barn on Loudon Avenue to the Phoenix Hotel. An old streetcar from the horse-drawn era was converted in 1892 to a passenger waiting station in the middle of West Main Street at Cheapside. "Lexington is certainly on a boom," a local newspaper trumpeted.[27]

Well, not quite. In other ways, Lexington remained the same sleepy city it had been for as long as anyone could remember. Snake oil salesmen still turned up to sell their patent medicines at Cheapside, a sure sign of spring, as the *Morning Herald* remarked in 1896. Buggy accidents still occurred, because people still transported themselves by horse and buggy. H. P. Kelly, well known as a horseman, was injured after suffering a convulsive fit while at the reins of a team of high-spirited horses near Sixth Street. He pitched headlong out of the buggy, and the horses ran down Broadway nearly to Third Street, where someone caught them. Livery stables downtown continued to pose safety hazards. One stable opened right onto the sidewalk of a busy street, creating a hazard when horses went in or out. The entrance was "either filthy or blocked by a load of hay or an old horse standing in front of it," the *Kentucky Leader* reported in 1890, adding, "the ladies, in order to pass, are compelled to walk out in the street." The Town Branch remained a major sanitation problem. In 1890, Councilman Treacy complained about the common practice of running sewer lines directly into the creek, "allowing it to become offensive and a source of disease in the thickly settled part of the city."[28]

But slowly, if reluctantly in some quarters, Lexington was inching closer to modernity. The city authorized the laying of brick on East Main Street from Walnut Street to the city limits. West Main received brick from Broadway to Cox Street. Short Street was bricked between North Limestone Street and Walnut. The city was bursting at its boundaries, with the Belt Land Co. developing acreage between Broadway and Winchester Pike. Developers, most of them local residents, had seen to dividing and platting the land into residential lots. Grading of streets began in the new development. "The ground is high and is beyond question the most charming location for residence property in the suburbs of Lexington," read an account in the *Kentucky Leader*.[29] Lexington was on the move.

Changes had begun bringing more newcomers to the Bluegrass. John E. Madden was thirty years old in 1886 when he arrived in Kentucky. He was born December 28, 1856, in Bethlehem, Pennsylvania, where the sparks and pollution that spewed in dark plumes from ubiquitous smokestacks bespoke the industrial age that defined Madden's youth. His parents, Patrick and Catherine McKee Madden, were Irish immigrants from Roscommon County—the same origin as Councilman Treacy's family. Madden's father labored in the zinc works of Bethlehem before his death in 1860. If young Madden had been an ordinary teenager, he might have followed the majority of townsfolk into the Pennsylvania coal mines or the factory of Bethlehem Steel. But he was no ordinary young man, as the horse world would soon discover.[30]

Madden grew up as an athlete. He excelled at baseball and track. He ran foot races at county fairs throughout Pennsylvania. At these fairs, he learned to ride and drive horses. He was winning trotting races before he was sixteen. He saved enough money to buy his first trotter, traded it for another, and made this a pattern and business model he would follow throughout his life. When he wasn't running foot races or trading trotters, always for a better horse, Madden won a few dollars here and there in boxing matches. He also learned to gamble.[31]

With his increasing success in the trotting horse business, Madden decided Kentucky was the place he needed to be. He moved into the Phoenix Hotel—the horsemen's headquarters, as the hotel advertised—and within two years began to deal in Thoroughbreds. His most important purchase of a Thoroughbred would be a weanling colt sired by Hanover that he bought in 1895 for $1,200 and named Hamburg. Madden trained Hamburg to a championship season at age two, and then sold him for $40,001 to Marcus Daly, copper king of Montana. Madden turned right around and paid $30,000 for 235 acres on the Winchester Pike, calling it Hamburg Place. "I wanted a place near town so, if I had a customer, I could get him out there before he changed his mind," Madden said. During his early years at Hamburg Place, Madden kept both trotting stock and Thoroughbreds. The farm grew to some 2,000 acres within a dozen years. (In the later twentieth century, it became the nucleus for a shopping mall by the same name.)[32]

Madden won the Kentucky Derby once as an owner and five additional times as a breeder, including in 1919 with Sir Barton, the first winner of the Triple Crown in the United States. (His grandson, Preston Madden, bred the sixth Kentucky Derby winner foaled at Hamburg Place, Alysheba, which won the race in 1987.) John Madden reportedly brought into the sport William Collins Whitney, a lawyer in New York who later served as secretary of the navy under President Grover Cleveland. Whitney's wealth came from his involvement in the consolidation of the transit system in New York City, his role in the founding of the American Tobacco Company, and his interests in an electric company later known as Consolidated Edison. Madden trained Whitney's winner of the 1900 Futurity, Ballyhoo Bey. Madden was a brilliant trainer (inducted into the National Museum of Racing and Hall of Fame in 1983), a shrewd horse salesman, and an authority on the care of horses. It is tempting to picture him kicking around the Phoenix Hotel before he grew wealthy and famous, lounging in the small office of William "George Wilkes" Simmons, talking trotters with George Singerly, with Robert Bonner and his son, Allie, and with J. Malcolm Forbes.

But Madden could also see what was coming in the early twentieth century as Thoroughbred racing began to eclipse the popularity of the harness sport. He slowly but wisely diversified into Thoroughbred racing, a move that brought him into a larger world of big money. Meantime, the trotting world began a contraction that was not entirely a result of the Panic of 1893. The time was fast approaching when the automobile would roll the road-driving sport off the highways and into oblivion. Trotters and pacers would be confined to racetracks. Despite some up and down years, Thoroughbred racing would be the sport to experience real growth.

The first automobile seen in Lexington was built and owned by Mr. Thomas B. Dewhurst in 1899. Pryor, the physician, wrote in his memoir: "A few years later he sold a one-cylinder Cadillac to Major Alex Morgan. It was an open car, no top, the door in the rear, and two steps for getting in. You could hear the 'chug-chug' of the engine for some distance."[33] Major Morgan was considerate as he chug-chugged along in his horseless carriage down the macadam road. When he saw a horse approaching, he would stop his automobile so as not to frighten the animal. But not every driver was as thoughtful. Horses and these newfangled horseless carriages were not going to fare well going down the same roads simultaneously, as everyone could see.

Many who still rode or drove horses resented this new diversion of the wealthy, who were taking up road space with their automobiles. Pryor recalled events of an automobile trip from Lexington to Maysville: "On our way to Maysville, when we were beyond Paris, we saw a man go out on the road and walk around. Major drove around this spot, got out and picked up a number of tacks the man had thrown in the road."[34] A lot of people regarded the horseless carriage not only as a nuisance but as a passing fad. No way would it last.

Belle Brezing would have seen and welcomed these changes. A brilliant businesswoman, she sensed big money coming to her town.

chapter **NINE**

Crackdown on Vice

The big money came to town in the pockets of a mining king, James Ben Ali Haggin. Lexington was not prepared for the likes of Haggin when he purchased Elmendorf Farm in 1897. This modest horse and tobacco town, which came awake only seasonally with the fall trots and tobacco auctions, slumbered the rest of the year beneath a comforting blanket of parochial vision and insular ways. The very idea of an outsider constructing a forty-room mansion of marble and natural stone would have seemed beyond belief in the Bluegrass—until Haggin, with his millions of dollars, worth billions today, built the house as a wedding present for his young bride, Pearl Voorhies. He was seventy-six. She was twenty-eight.[1]

Belle Brezing would come to rue the day that Haggin came to Lexington, for he enabled the rise of a former federal bureaucrat named Charles Berryman. Berryman used the power of his position as manager of Elmendorf to assume a voice of authority in the business community. When the twentieth century entered its second decade, Berryman would start advocating a new moral code for Lexington. He would go after Belle Brezing and all of Megowan Street with a vengeance.

Lexington knew Haggin only from a distance. He was rarely in residence at Elmendorf, in northwestern Fayette County. Citizens of the city acquired their familiarity with his name mostly from newspaper accounts, for his name appeared frequently and not always in a complimentary way. He and Pearl made their home on Fifth Avenue in New York, visiting Elmendorf and its mansion, which they named Green Hills, only a few weeks each year.

At first, their marriage shocked central Kentucky. Pearl was from Versailles and a cousin to Haggin's deceased wife, Eliza Jane Sanders. The couple's age difference scandalized the local population. So did the suddenness of the nuptials. Haggin announced their betrothal the night before they married. He had spent the past year denying they might marry. Pearl married Haggin in defiance of her parents' wishes.

But the Haggins soon won the hearts of Lexington society. They invited local gentry to dine and dance at Elmendorf to orchestras Haggin brought in from New York. Those invited to these soirees saw the softer side of Haggin, who played the role of congenial host.[2]

The larger world knew another side of Haggin, as an industrialist who owned a string of mines from Alaska to Chile. Born in Harrodsburg, Kentucky, Haggin graduated from Centre College in Danville and practiced law for brief periods in Shelbyville and in St. Joseph, Missouri, Natchez, Mississippi, and New Orleans before heading to California in 1850. Haggin realized his fortune not in law but in mine ownership. When clients failed to pay their legal bills, he accepted shares in their mines as payment. At first, Haggin's shares were almost worthless. But Haggin was an extraordinarily lucky man who became an extraordinarily wealthy one when the value of his mining stocks skyrocketed. He expanded his mining interests to a string of some 160 gold, silver, and copper mines extending from the northwestern United States through the length of South America.[3]

Everything Haggin touched turned to gold. When American cities began acquiring electricity in the 1890s, Haggin and his partners in California, Lloyd Tevis and Senator George Hurst, stood poised to enhance their fortunes exponentially. They owned the Anaconda mine, one of the world's richest sources of copper sulfur. When manufactured into wire, this copper carried electricity into American homes and businesses. With the coming of electricity, the price of copper skyrocketed. Haggin, Tevis, and Hurst were American success stories writ large.[4]

The world also knew Haggin as owner of the world's largest racing stable. He owned about a thousand racehorses. He kept another thousand head of breeding stock on his Rancho del Paso near Sacramento, California. Rancho del Paso rose out of the desert as a testament to the miracle of irrigation. Never mind that Haggin had diverted the Kern River to construct his farm. In fact, he angered numerous ranchers by altering the flow of water away from their grazing land to his property. On his newly irrigated land, Haggin built a horse-breeding empire unlike anything previously seen in the United States.

Haggin was reserved, taciturn, and unpopular with his business peers. He also was fully capable of wielding his wealth like a heavy bludgeon when he wanted his way. On Kentucky Derby day in 1886, he became enraged when he discovered that Churchill Downs had locked out the on-track bookmakers in a contract dispute over licensing fees. This meant Haggin had no way to get a bet down on his horse, Ben Ali, who wound up winning the Derby. The $4,890 winner's purse meant little to Haggin. He wanted to experience the rush of a greater thrill by betting on his horse. Haggin tried every way to get the bookmakers back on track. He offered a personal donation to make up the difference between the amount in licensing fees the track demanded from the bookmakers and what they had paid in the past. At the last minute, Churchill Downs reluctantly relented. Twenty-three bookmakers stood ready to take Haggin's money by the time Ben Ali went to the post. But track officials resented this wealthy man's meddling. "Who did Haggin think he was?" one track official asked. Well, Haggin showed them who he *knew* he was.

The very next day, Haggin ordered all of his horses at Churchill Downs loaded on the train. He departed Louisville, vowing never to return. Moreover, he swore he would speak to his friends in New York racing and encourage them to boycott the Derby. And Haggin may have had the clout to do it. With one exception, Mike Dwyer in 1896, the major racing stables did not send their horses to the Derby for the next twenty-five years. This possibly had more to do with a lack of bookmakers and big betting money on the grounds than with Haggin's influence over other racing stables. But the coincidence does invite speculation about the power of this one man.[5]

Given his go-to-hell way of treating others, Haggin frequently came under fire. His success in the Thoroughbred auction arena drew criticism. Every year, he shipped trainloads of yearling Thoroughbreds to these sales in New York, first from Rancho del Paso and later also from Elmendorf. People accused him of trying to control the market by having his representatives join the bidding to run up the prices on his horses. The *Illustrated Sporting News* joined the firestorm, commenting that Haggin "endeavors to dispose of his yearlings in a manner that is disgusting to all men who seek fair play in the sale ring." Kentucky breeders were especially angry with Haggin. They expressed concern that horse buyers would think *all* Kentuckians engaged in this practice.[6]

Haggin's success in Thoroughbred racing had begun soon after he got into the sport in 1881. He was successful in great part because he sought the aid of Daniel Swigert, the man who founded Elmendorf Farm. Swigert had since sold the farm, but he continued to buy and sell Thoroughbreds. From Swigert, Haggin acquired his greatest racehorses: Ben Ali, Salvator, and Miss Woodford. Haggin also owned a champion filly named Firenze. Salvator, Miss Woodford, and Firenze ranked among the greatest names in sports during the latter part of the nineteenth century.

Haggin bought numerous properties in the neighborhood of Elmendorf, and the farm expanded to more than twelve thousand acres. Con J. Enright was the first to manage Elmendorf for Haggin. After his resignation in 1904, Charles H. Berryman took over the farm. The manager's post placed Berryman in an enviable position as unquestioned representative of the absent Haggin. Unlike Enright before him, Berryman used the power of his position to build a network of relationships reaching far into the community. The deference paid to Berryman in Lexington began preparing him for the role he would take on ten years later as defender of community morals. When this occurred, Berryman's powerful connections would clash with the influential network Belle had tended so carefully through the years.[7]

Dr. Charles A. Nevitt was another powerful man in Lexington, a physician and superintendent of Elmwood General Hospital on Leestown Pike. Nevitt began treating Belle after she developed an addiction to morphine, and she frequently sought his help to break her drug habit. She realized the drug's danger, having attempted suicide years earlier by taking a morphine overdose. James Tandy Ellis remembered Belle taking "the dope." "Belle was pleasant and would talk to you in a motherly sort of way at times when the dope was working smoothly." After the Harrison Narcotic Act went into effect in 1915, Belle made repeated attempts to break her drug habit. She would check into Nevitt's sanitarium at Elmwood General Hospital, where he would reduce her dose gradually until she would be taking very little morphine. However, Belle would begin to hemorrhage, Nevitt recalled, so he would have to increase her dose. Eventually he obtained permission from narcotics inspectors to prescribe for Belle all the morphine she needed. He described her as an incurable. He gave her prescriptions, and she administered the morphine herself.[8]

When the morphine dosage was adjusted right, Belle presented a glamorous picture as head of her famous brothel. Pink Thomas recalled Belle stopping by her house one day, dressed all in white. She was on her way to the bank. On another occasion, a man from Wichita, Kansas, who was in Lexington for the trots, asked Pink to go "hopping." Pink replied, "Alright, we'll go around to Miss Belle's." She knew the man was a big spender. Pink sent word to Belle to come downstairs because she wanted to introduce her to the man. "She came down with a whole handful of diamonds on," Pink said.[9] Each evening would find Belle in a room behind the main stairway of her house, reading a book in between greeting customers. She chose this room because it gave her a view of both the front and side doors.

One day, Eph Sayre's brother-in-law, D. D. Bell, came to Belle's house and told Clara Sayre, "My wife's out of town. Let's go to the house and I'll show you what a pretty little daughter I've got." He organized a group of Belle's prostitutes to visit his Bell House mansion (now a city-owned event space surrounded by the Bell Court neighborhood). "He called for his carriage and loaded it up with whores and took them to Bell House," Clara said. "The little girl was asleep in an upstairs room. So the whores all tiptoed in and looked at her. That was the little girl who grew up to be Clara Bell, perhaps the most popular and sought-after young woman in Lexington society."[10]

Trotting meets came and went through the years, always bringing more business to Belle's house. They brought the only racing action to Belle's from 1898 to 1905, when the Thoroughbred track was closed. "Miss Belle would have a ball during the trots," recalled a bartender in Lexington, John Coyne.[11]

Phil Chinn recalled a banker from Boston, Allie Baunta, arriving in Lexington prior to the trotting meet and renting Belle's house for the entire duration of the meet. Considering Belle's Singerly connection, this must have occurred after William Singerly's death in 1898, or George Singerly's in 1902. One night while Baunta held a lease on the house, Belle received a phone call from a horseman from Bourbon County, Warren Stoner. He was calling from the Phoenix Hotel and wanted to bring his friends up to the Hill to visit Belle. Stoner had just finished an oyster feast at the Phoenix. "He had oyster stew and then fried oysters," Chinn said. Belle, however, told him he could not visit her place because Baunta was in residence. Stoner refused to take no for an answer. He and his friends showed up at her door, but Belle would not let them in.[12]

Stoner went across the street to a brothel run by an African American woman, Mollie Irvine. Irvine installed Stoner and his eight guests in a parlor and sent in three prostitutes to entertain them. Stoner asked why Irvine could not come up with more than three whores. She told him the rest were dancing with other guests in her dance hall. Stoner insisted she call all the prostitutes into the room where he and his guests waited. He leased her house on the spot until the conclusion of the trotting meet, precisely the same time Baunta's lease would end at Belle's.[13]

Occasionally, Belle took her prostitutes to the Lexington Opera House. Their habit was to arrive just before curtain time, dressed conservatively but in the latest fashions. They would proceed immediately to a box from which they watched the show. Belle also took these women on shopping trips, but always after hours. She would telephone the proprietor of a women's apparel shop east of the Phoenix Hotel and ask that the store remain open past 5:30 p.m. As soon as the store closed to regular customers, Belle's carriage pulled up at the door, and the prostitutes went inside to shop. Belle always paid with a check.[14]

Belle's good friend Ernest Featherstone was still on the scene. In 1913 he suffered serious injuries in an automobile accident. A prominent veterinarian, Dr. Ed Hagyard, invited Featherstone to accompany him on a professional call to treat animals in Winchester. Hagyard was making the trip in his fast, new automobile. The men decided to take along another acquaintance, John Hussey. Hagyard told Hussey to take the wheel. Hagyard was proud of his fast car. On the way to Winchester, the veterinarian began to brag about the high speed his auto could attain. He asked Hussey to "let her step," and the car soon hit a fast thirty-five miles per hour. But it also hit a slick spot in the road. The car slid and then tipped over. Hussey escaped with a slight scalp wound. Hagyard received two broken ribs and bruises to his body. Featherstone suffered a serious head injury. Featherstone lingered at home for seven weeks. But toward the end of that time, he began to grow restless. He was missing the fall trotting meet. By week six, he could not keep still any longer. He began taking telephone calls from horsemen who called to keep him current on every race.[15]

Belle continued to send money for the support of her daughter, Daisy May. In 1894, Belle had taken her out of school in Newport, Kentucky, and sent her to live in Detroit with the Sisters of the Good Shepherd. The nuns operated a refuge for women named the House of the Good Shepherd. The nuns changed Daisy May's name upon her arrival from Daisy Barnett to Imelda Kinney, a misspelling of Belle's married name, Kenney. (The nun keeping the records had terrible handwriting, which probably explained the misspelling.) In the beginning, the nuns placed Daisy with a younger group, most of them orphans and abused girls. Daisy May could not read or write. She had no job assignment at the institution, although most of the other girls did. Fourteen years later, in 1908, the Sisters of the Good Shepherd moved Daisy May into a group of older women. These were women who had been in some kind of trouble or who had no resources to care for themselves. The person responsible for Daisy May was identified as Mrs. J. B. Kenney, box 39, Lexington, Kentucky. The U.S. Census for Detroit in 1910 listed Daisy Kenney, then about thirty years old, as born in Kentucky and living at the institution. Daisy May would remain in institutions the rest of her life.[16]

Belle's world was nearing a collision with Berryman's. A wave of antiprostitution sentiment was building in Lexington, similar to reform movements unfolding in nearly every major American city in the years leading up to the First World War. The heat from reformers was becoming more intense than it had been when Belle's neighbors ran her out of North Upper Street. Berryman would be a central character in a new reform wave aimed at the women on the Hill.

Social reform acquired great cachet with the middle class beginning with Theodore Roosevelt's presidency in 1901. This was the beginning of the Progressive Era, or the Age of Reform, as some have called it. Progressives believed the United States was failing its citizens by paying more attention to big business and big money than to average folk. They saw a need to change conditions in many areas of American life, from the workplace to the nation's dwindling supply of natural wilderness. Progressives fought for federal inspection of meatpacking plants and federal control of food and drugs. They broke up the monopolies of the big railroad conglomerates. They fought for a progressive income tax and direct election of senators. Progressives also went after saloons, gambling, and red-light districts. They believed these three "evils" were ruinous to family life.

Beginning in 1901 in Lexington, nearly every grand jury report to the Fayette Circuit Court bore a Progressive stamp. Grand juries recommended closing saloons on Sundays. They opposed gambling, particularly slot machines. By 1908, grand juries in Fayette County had turned their attention to prostitution after the discovery of numerous "assignation houses" operating in residential neighborhoods. This 1908 report indicated that the court had become concerned with a proliferation of prostitution outside the bounds of the red-light district. For the time being, the houses on Megowan and surrounding streets remained free from grand jury purview. Over the next few years, this would change.[17]

A few crusaders had complained about prostitution in downtown Lexington since at least the 1870s. They continued to do so even after most brothels relocated to the red-light district beginning about 1890. But those early crusaders were outliers, a minority of righteous folk whose voices were overpowered by the powerful connections linking brothel operators with city authorities and boss government.

When the new wave of antiprostitution reformers emerged nationwide after 1900, the general population did not agree immediately that red-light districts should close. Change came slowly over the seventeen years before American involvement in World War I. Victorians had characterized prostitution as a "necessary evil" in society that probably was best handled by segregating prostitutes into red-light districts. Progressives came to see prostitution as a "social evil" that needed to be stamped out. Sociologist Ruth Rosen called this cultural turn a watershed. Americans of the Progressive Era, according to Rosen, were "horrified" by the "large-scale commercialization and rationalization of prostitution by third-party agents," which included landlords renting to madams, police and politicians, physicians who examined and treated prostitutes, liquor merchants who enjoyed a lucrative business in red-light districts, and even cab drivers who delivered fares to these resorts of ill fame.[18]

In Lexington, Fayette Circuit Court grand juries convened on a regular schedule several times a year. The court empanelled these groups of citizens and charged them with determining whether persons charged by police with crimes should be indicted and tried in circuit court. Each grand jury also issued a report in which these citizens pointed to specific areas of concern in Lexington or Fayette County.

In 1910, a grand jury moved a routine investigation of prostitution closer to the boundaries of the red-light district by taking a serious look at Dewees Street, just two blocks west of Megowan. Citizens had expressed concern because many people used Dewees Street to reach downtown from residential developments in northeast Lexington. People looking out the streetcar windows on Dewees expressed disgust at the whorehouses in plain view. The inhabitants of these houses sat on their porches, skirts halfway up to their knees, shouting out possibilities of what might lie inside the houses. Belle herself had called the police to complain about this very practice creeping onto Megowan Street. She thought it cheapened the neighborhood, and she insisted that police put an end to this disgrace. She did not allow her women to sit on her porch, and she did not want to see prostitutes behaving this way at any other house on her street.[19]

Belle was fighting a losing battle in trying to maintain high standards of decorum. The red-light district was slipping into decline. Shockingly to Belle, the women of the district were behaving like whores. Moreover, they no longer appeared content to stay within the district. A Megowan Street madam turned up in police court in 1913 to pay the fine for a woman arrested for street fighting. Police Chief J. J. Reagan expressed frustration with whores literally "hopping the fence." "Megowan Street is going to look respectable even if it is not," the chief announced. "Any proprietor who cannot keep her girls indoors and well-behaved will have to close up and move out." Reagan said the whores had been causing too much trouble lately in restaurants and lunchrooms downtown. From now on, if women from Megowan Street wanted something to eat, they could go into the kitchens of the bawdy houses where they lived and cook something. "A little domesticity will be a good thing in that district," Reagan said.[20]

Some forward-thinking citizens, realizing that the double standard for men's and women's morality stood in the way of shutting down prostitution, convened a mass meeting in 1913 to discuss the issue. The meeting was to be held at the Ben Ali Theater, built by Haggin as one of several investments he made in downtown real estate. Berryman had been actively involved in construction of the theater, and he approved its use for this meeting.[21]

Between grand jury reports, which were denouncing prostitution at a fairly regular pace now, the fun continued on Megowan Street. Belle decided to give her girls a special surprise on Christmas morning of 1912. Many years in the future, John Jacob Niles would enjoy world-wide fame as a balladeer, folk singer, and musician, but in 1912 he was a struggling twenty-year-old playing piano in a saloon on South Lime-stone Street near Main Street. He received a call from a woman he identified as "the most widely known madam in all our area" wishing to organize a music performance at her house.[22]

Niles walked to Belle's house and raised the silver knocker on the door. When he was admitted, Belle got right to the point. She told Niles she wanted to hire a quartet of two men and two women to sing "the Christmas hymns or whatever they are called." Belle promised $20 and a hearty Christmas breakfast. Before Niles could make up his mind, a pretty, blonde young woman walked into the room. Niles took a long look at her breasts, which were plainly visible. "They were small," he wrote in a memoir, "because she was a small girl. The breasts were posi-tively beautiful, nipples on the pink side, she being a blond."[23]

His first thought was that Belle was trying to influence his judg-ment by trotting out a whore to charm him. Belle noticed how fasci-nated Niles was with the young girl's bosom, and the girl was aware, too. She smiled. Then she said, "I'm sorry to interrupt you, Miss Belle, but I cannot get Billy Carson out of my bed. He won't wake up. He is still breathing, but, well, I am not strong enough to drag that fat swine out of my bed."[24]

Niles didn't manage to put together a quartet, but on Christmas morning at Belle's house he performed ten carols a cappella, including one he wrote that would later become famous: "Jesus, Jesus, Rest Your Head." Belle made good on her promise to serve breakfast. "From time to time," Niles said, "the girls, now dressed quite like great ladies, came timidly and ate ravenously, giggled like boarding school girls and, along with some excellent food, devoured me with their eyes." When it was over, Belle rose from the table and everyone else followed suit. Belle escorted Niles to the door and handed him his pay envelope, which contained not the promised $20 but $25, a fortune for a young saloon singer.[25]

Belle would not have many more opportunities to arrange such a memorable fete at her Megowan Street house. Elements in the city were determined to shut down prostitution. Additional grand jury reports pointed to the proliferation of the trade in various parts of the city. A 1911 report had even complained about the sale of alcoholic beverages, in particular to minors, in the red-light district. The watershed report appeared in November 1913, making big headlines in the *Lexington Herald:* "Grand Jury Advises Obliteration of the Red Light District." Clearly, Lexington citizens were now telling authorities they no longer wished to tolerate prostitution anywhere in the city, not even in the district where brothels had traditionally been permitted to operate.[26]

With the 1913 grand jury report came a long list of indictments against madams and landlords, all but a few operating on Megowan Street. Belle was indicted for "keeping and conducting a bawdy house at 153 Megowan Street" (the house numbers had changed in 1902) and for "selling liquor without a license." A landlord named Gustave Luigart was named in ten indictments, all for renting houses to various madams operating on Megowan Street. Luigart was a popular businessman who for sixteen years had owned and operated a restaurant on West Short Street called the English Kitchen. James Foley received four indictments for the same reason Luigart had. Even former Judge John J. Riley, longtime friend to Lexington's whores, was indicted "for renting a house to Lizzie Davidson at 161 Megowan Street."[27]

A new group of citizens concerned about prostitution had formed in 1913, calling itself the Temporary Committee on Social Hygiene. This committee planned to attack prostitution through science and education. The group announced a public meeting at the YMCA for December, where it would lay out a campaign to add sex education to the curriculum in the public schools. The logic was simple. The social hygiene proponents believed that by educating young people about sex and the dangers of disease, they could train young boys and girls to resist temptations in the streets. The committee reported that prostitutes were stepping outside their district boundaries and assailing young boys, while also posing dangers to young girls. Only sex education would prepare these youth to resist the lure of the bawdy houses.

One example was the case of Annie Parker, a fourteen-year-old girl "lured" to the home of a Megowan Street madam, Pearl Yates. The girl had arrived in town from the mountains. She said she did not know the character of Pearl Yates's house when she stopped there. For her part, the madam insisted she did not entice the girl to her house. Police learned about the girl when a saloonkeeper familiar with her family made a complaint. Yates went to jail while awaiting trial, and the girl was given into the custody of juvenile authorities.[28]

Robberies and assaults on Megowan Street were beginning to receive closer attention as well. Fayette Circuit judge Charles Kerr declared from the bench that the red-light district was a spawning ground for crime. Truthfully, crime was not new to the neighborhood. A young farmer, in Lexington to sell livestock in 1897, was robbed of $450 in the backyard of a house there. He suffered a severe beating. Similar crimes were reported from the district through the years. A particularly busy month on Megowan Street was January 1911: a double shooting, a stabbing, and a guilty verdict for a man who shot and killed his prostitute wife.[29] But the crime rate did appear to be increasing. This was not the Megowan Street of Belle Brezing's glory days.

The place was going to hell in a hurry, and no one realized this more than Belle. One night in July 1911, the police answered a call from her house. They walked in to find a murder scene. A young man named Oliver Broaddus had fatally stabbed a beautiful, red-haired prostitute, twenty-two years old, using the alias of Alice Ely. Her real name was Debbie Harvey. Belle had attempted to pull Broaddus off the woman, but then had to run in fear for her life when Broaddus turned on her. Then Broaddus fled the house.[30]

Police thought they had found his trail when they discovered blood leading from Belle's house down Wilson, Short, and Walnut streets. But the trail of blood did not lead to Broaddus; it turned out to belong to another man who had been in a room with a girl when he heard the screams. With the entire house in pandemonium, the man leaped through a window to escape and cut himself on the glass. Broaddus, it turned out, had gone into hiding in a slaughterhouse on Old Frankfort

Pike, across from the Pepper Distillery. He turned himself in to police the following day. Months later, when tried in court, a jury found him not guilty by reason of insanity. Shortly afterward, he escaped from the lunatic asylum on Fourth Street.[31]

Then Charles Berryman entered the antivice fray in a big way. His employer, James Ben Ali Haggin, the mining king who had given Lexington a vicarious glimpse at big money, died on September 12, 1914, at age ninety-three. Berryman stayed on at Elmendorf to manage the farm for Haggin's estate. He joined a number of lawyers, businessmen, and physicians in forming a new group of concerned citizens, which they named the Fayette Co-operative Association. This group made an appeal to city government to form a vice commission.[32]

Berryman and his colleagues were able to put quite a lot of pressure on the city to act. The Fayette Co-operative Association included many influential men willing to use their power to persuade the municipal government to move forward. Under pressure, the city appointed a vice commission in 1915, headed by the pastor of Christ Church Cathedral, Dean Massie. Berryman, who served on various local boards including the Fayette County Board of Education, accepted an appointment to this commission. Other members included the Reverend Charles Lee Reynolds, pastor of the Second Presbyterian Church; Mrs. A. M. Harrison, chairman of the Department of Social Hygiene in the Kentucky Federation of Women's Clubs; J. E. Bassett, a merchant and president of the Fayette National Bank; Dr. Samuel H. Halley, president of the Fayette Leaf Tobacco Warehouse Company; Mrs. George R. Hunt, vice president of the Orphan's Association; Judge W. T. Lafferty, dean of the law faculty of State University (later the University of Kentucky); Dr. John W. Scott, a physician; and George S. Shanklin, a lawyer and president of the Fayette Home Telephone Company.[33]

The vice commission moved quickly on its agenda. It brought in experts from the American Social Hygiene Association to share information. The vice president of this national group was Jane Addams, founder of Hull House, a settlement house created to uplift the lives of women and children living in Chicago's slums. At a meeting held at the YMCA building, Dr. J. A. Stucky declared red-light districts a failure because the system of segregating prostitutes led only to graft. He condemned saloons, gambling, and brothels as "the Devil's trinity."[34]

Lexington citizens, like most other Americans, were taking a long, hard look at the fabric binding their moral and social culture. Belle, hounded out of one neighborhood nearly a quarter-century earlier, must have wondered what lay ahead for her life on Megowan Street.

chapter **TEN**

A Growing Moral Menace

Most madams and whores carried on their business atop the Hill as though antiprostitution efforts were not gaining support. Shut down the red-light district? It could never happen, they thought. The frolicking good times continued every night and into the early mornings on Megowan Street. The whores and their keepers, along with the liquor merchants, the landlords, and even the stores that rented furniture to the brothels, believed business would continue forever.

Belle had more to think about than how the community's moral awakening might change her life. In March 1913, eight months before the watershed grand jury report, the nuns in Detroit had moved Daisy May to another institution. Accompanied by a Sister Marie Theresa, Daisy May moved into the St. Joseph Retreat in Dearborn, not far from Detroit. She was accepted for residency on May 27. A nun belonging to the order of the Sisters of the Good Shepherd suggested that the ten-week interval between arrival and the official start of residency probably was a probationary period. Daisy May now was thirty-seven years old.[1]

Belle was fifty-three. She needed to start thinking about her future and what this new attitude sweeping through Lexington might mean for Megowan Street. One or the other of the Singerlys had left her a wealthy woman. She did not need to continue working. She could close down her house and travel to Europe if she wished. Still, despite grim prospects on the horizon, Belle did not retire. Perhaps Belle's drive to work came from a deep need she could not have fully explained. Memories of what it had been like to scrounge for a living in the streets long ago may have scarred her so deeply that she never could rest comfortably with her wealth. The fear of falling backward may have pushed her always forward. Perhaps she could not rest.

Just as likely, Belle enjoyed the camaraderie of whorehouse life. She liked the company of her favorite clients. And these clients would not have wanted her to close her business. For all of these years, they had enjoyed relaxing in Belle's company, meeting friends in what amounted to a private club, sipping spirits and making their horse deals on familiar turf. Belle's house was integral to their culture, to their lifestyle, and to whatever notions they entertained in their imaginations about living a squire's life in the Old South. None among her regulars would have wanted to see this change.

But changes were occurring in Lexington, and these in turn would bring changes to Megowan Street. The city was becoming more modern. When Belle had opened for business on Megowan Street more than thirty years earlier, the streets echoed with the sound of horses' hooves pulling streetcars and buggies. Now automobiles pulled up to Belle's front door. The acrid smell of gasoline replaced the aroma of warm manure dropped on city streets. Change often sparks in many people a nostalgic longing for the better days. Men could still slip back to those days at Miss Belle's.

Automobiles were bringing the greatest changes to Lexington. Those who could afford a motorized vehicle were switching from horses and buggies as quickly as they could purchase a car. The city government took a big step in 1911, voting to purchase two motor-driven fire trucks. The city had debated making this move for two years since Fire Chief W. A. Jesse first made his pitch in 1909. City commissioners were reluctant to let the horses go, but as the chief explained the economics, it began to make sense. Motorized fire trucks would be faster, he told the commissioners, with speeds of thirty-five to forty miles per hour, as opposed to the horses' ten to fifteen. The motorized trucks would not tire as horses sometimes did on the way to a fire. They would require gasoline only when in use, whereas horses needed to be fed every day whether they went to a fire or not.[2]

Lexington hardly resembled its former self. Major real estate developments had begun during the later 1800s, with subdivisions going up everywhere: Woodward Heights, platted in 1887, embraced parts of High, Maxwell, and Pine streets; Herr Park, platted in 1893, encompassed land west of South Limestone Street and included Transcript, Gazette, Leader, and Press avenues. Who among the old-timers could have dreamed Lexington would reach to where the University of Kentucky Hospital now stands, much less far beyond it? Elsmere Park in north Lexington was platted in 1890 into sixty lots with boundaries at Broadway, Seventh, Sixth, and Upper streets. Many more developments than these had been platted, and new homes were popping up all over the expanding city. Lexington was quickly growing large and modern.

The horse business, which had struggled since the Civil War, was bringing greater financial returns every year. A yearling Thoroughbred brought on average only about $500 at auction, but this was much better than the $200 average realized decades earlier. The number of wealthy outsiders buying farmland also was rising. In 1912, Claiborne Farm joined this growing list of new farms. Arthur Hancock, who had been in charge of Ellerslie Farm in Virginia for his father, Captain Richard Johnson Hancock, had married a Kentuckian, Nancy Clay, in 1908. Beginning in 1910, the younger Hancock operated Clay's family farm in Bourbon County simultaneously with Ellerslie. This resulted in a lot of traveling between Virginia and Kentucky. Hancock and his wife solved that problem when they moved to the Kentucky farm in 1912, setting Claiborne Farm on its historic course to becoming a premier farm globally.[3]

Hancock brought a new energy to the modern era of Thoroughbred breeding. He was an innovator and a risk taker whose big-stakes gambles included the syndication of major stallion prospects, something not entirely new but novel on the financial level at which Hancock dealt. His integrity was unquestioned. People with big money trusted him. The farm acquired some of the world's leading stallions and a first-class client list.

Wealthy outsiders were contributing increasingly to a more cosmopolitan landscape, and all were bringing new ideas to Lexington along with their money. One of the most fascinating characters during Belle's lifetime was Edward R. Bradley. He bought 336 acres in 1906 on the old Frankfort Pike, naming his estate Idle Hour Farm. Bradley was exceedingly wealthy, enjoying a fortune he had accumulated by developing a fancy gambling casino in Palm Beach, Florida. He, like Haggin, was a self-made man.

While Bradley was young, he worked numerous jobs that did not portend making a fortune. These included laboring in a steel mill in Pennsylvania and then working as a dishwasher. Bradley liked to keep on the move. He worked in Texas as a cowboy. He worked as an Indian scout and prospected for gold. Once he acquired the money to set up his Florida casino he initiated dress rules, just as Belle Brezing had in her house. Bradley required his customers to wear evening dress after 7:00 p.m. Bradley's clients were high rollers who had to at least look first class.[4]

Over his lifetime, Bradley expanded Idle Hour Farm to 1,292 acres. He won the Kentucky Derby four times, with horses whose names all began with the letter B: Behave Yourself, Bubbling Over, Burgoo King, and Broker's Tip. He never was ashamed of the way he had accumulated his fortune. Called to testify at a congressional hearing on gambling, Bradley answered "gambler" to the question of how he made his living. Bradley told the congressmen he would bet on anything and everything.

Bradley undoubtedly made the acquaintance of Kinzea Stone, a contemporary who had lived at various times in Bourbon County, Lexington, and finally Georgetown, where he opened a grocery store and eventually served as mayor. Stone won the Kentucky Derby in 1891 with Kingman. He also owned trotters and named a tobacco factory he owned after one of the fastest, most famous trotters: Maud S.[5]

Stone also invested in a venture to manufacture automobiles in Lexington. The company, the Lexington Motor Car Company, employed a clever advertising slogan suitable to the Bluegrass: "Bred in Old Kentucky." Stone designed one of the fancy sedans built in Lexington and purchased this automobile—they called it a limousine—in 1910. His granddaughter described road trips in the family's new car: "The tires weren't very strong, and the roads were unpaved. There were horses and buggies on the road, and the horses would shy. Even more would run away."[6]

Soon afterward, the Harkness family of Walnut Hall Farm purchased a custom-built sedan manufactured in Lexington. The Harknesses, heirs to the Standard Oil fortune, no longer made their way to the trotting track in a stylish coach pulled by four high-stepping horses—they drove to the track in their new automobile.[7]

Trotting fans were still stepping high with memories of that amazing afternoon in 1905 when a pacer named Dan Patch had set a 1:55¼ world record at Lexington's trotting track. Dan Patch was an American hero in the purest sense: born of humble beginnings, the horse rose to a life of fame and riches. Americans grabbed up all kinds of marketing memorabilia created to commemorate his career: Dan Patch washing machines, Dan Patch chewing tobacco, Dan Patch cigars, and even a Dan Patch automobile, priced at $525. The speed record the pacer set in Lexington would stand for thirty-three years, nearly the span of Belle's remaining years.[8]

Thoroughbred fans likewise felt good about their sport. The Kentucky Association track was to reopen in 1905 for the first time in eight years. Captain S. S. Brown, a Pittsburgh steel magnate, had rescued the track from financial despair, purchasing the racecourse in 1904 for $35,000. Over the next year, Brown spent an estimated $200,000 making the place presentable, for it had fallen into disrepair. "From dilapidated ruins the buildings have been converted into most comfortable quarters," read a newspaper account. "New barns, new fencing, new paddocks, new offices, new furniture, new roadways, new paving—the plant is now the best its size in America, complete in every detail, lacking nothing that the thought of its management could devise." Shouts of "They're off!" went up at 2:45 p.m. May 3, 1905. More than eight thousand Thoroughbred fans attended the races on opening day.[9]

Unfortunately, the immediate future of Thoroughbred racing in Lexington would not remain secure. Brown died seven months later, on December 11, 1905. His brother, Captain W. Harry Brown, was coexecutor of the estate with the Union Trust Company of Pittsburgh, and he did not express interest in owning a racetrack.[10]

Still another white knight rode into town, giving hope to local residents that he would save Thoroughbred racing. Colonel Matt Winn of Louisville took an option for a one-year lease on the association track. Winn was well known in racing. He had joined other investors in purchasing the struggling Churchill Downs in 1902. His ambition from that point on was to lure the country's top three-year-olds to the Derby, which meant he needed to convince the major New York racing stables that the race was not the backwater sporting event Haggin had said it was.

People in Lexington knew that if Winn exercised his option to lease their track, then the financial situation would still be tight. Winn could not bring the money to Lexington that Brown had. Consequently, rumors began to circulate that the track might have to cut costs by ending its longtime policy of complimentary passes for women. Even if Belle Brezing ever received a complimentary pass, she and her prostitutes now might have to pay to attend the races. "At the races the girls stayed to themselves and sent their bets down to the handbooks," said Coyne, the Lexington bartender.[11]

Winn looked around in 1906, talked to some dealmakers, but in the end chose not to get involved in the Lexington track. Nonetheless, local dealmakers organized a spring meet under the ownership of Brown's estate. This was possible only with considerable financial help from Lexington horsemen and businessmen. But by the following year, Winn was back, now at the helm as part of a new ownership group. Another member of this group was headed for a career as a U.S. senator: Johnson N. Camden of Versailles.[12]

Racing resumed in Lexington just as racetracks throughout the country were shutting down. The Progressives were winning their fight against gambling in numerous states, most notably New York. Thoroughbred racing in New York shut down in 1910, and tracks remained closed until 1913. In Lexington, Thoroughbred racing had critics, but the city avoided losing the sport. This happened because of some quick thinking by the Bluegrass power structure. These people, largely horsemen, organized a state racing commission that Governor John Crepps Wickliffe Beckham signed into law in 1906. Under the rule of this commission, the sport was to be conducted at the highest level of honesty. This was especially important during an age of reform when order and sound organization of any business held cachet. The Kentucky Association track did not close again until 1933, when it shut down forever, a victim once again of financial difficulties.[13]

By the time the racetrack closed, Belle would be seventy-three years old and a recluse in her house on Megowan Street. But during the century's second decade, when Thoroughbred racing at the Lexington track resumed, Belle was facing the biggest challenge in her life: a groundswell of public support for shutting down prostitution. The popular mood in Lexington clearly had changed from toleration to a desire to see the city cleared of prostitution. The numbers looked alarming:

158 brothels and saloons were flourishing in Lexington, according to one grand jury report. The year 1915 rolled around with Rev. Massie's vice commission, Berryman included, conducting a major investigation of the red-light district.

For a brief respite, a Thoroughbred filly named Regret turned everyone's attention to Churchill Downs. On May 8, she became the first of her gender to win the Kentucky Derby after fourteen fillies before had tried and failed. The man who trained Regret, James Rowe Sr., was no stranger to the Derby winner's circle. He had won the 1881 Derby with Hindoo, back in those horse-and-buggy days when Belle Brezing worked at Jennie Hill's place.

Regret was born and raised in New Jersey. Her owner, Harry Payne Whitney of New York, typified the wealthy outsiders buying up Bluegrass farmland for horse-breeding operations. Whitney's new farm was under development on a portion of the former Elmendorf. The man who would manage Whitney's horses in Kentucky was none other than Berryman, also hard at work on the vice commission.[14]

In an ironic twist, Whitney, while developing a horse operation on a portion of the former Haggin estate, was winning the very race that Haggin had sworn twenty-nine years ago to boycott forever. But Whitney's sending Regret from the East to win the race marked a turning point, one that Haggin would not have liked. Whitney's win led the way for additional wealthy New York turf men to begin supporting the Kentucky Derby. Matt Winn identified this watershed moment in his memoirs.

When Regret became the first filly to win the Kentucky Derby, the race began to receive much more national attention than it had in the past. Regret's win was ironic and unexpected, for as late as the day preceding this Derby, it was questionable that she would run. Her status lay in limbo because a passenger ship named the *Lusitania* sank off the coast of Ireland the day before the Derby, torpedoed by a German submarine. Among the 1,198 people killed was Whitney's brother-in-law, Alfred Gwynne Vanderbilt. The *Lusitania* tragedy would take its place on a long list of grievances that eventually saw the United States join World War I.

Whitney arrived in Louisville for the Derby with the question of Regret's status on everyone's mind. Would he pull the filly out of the race out of respect for his brother-in-law's death? The filly's trainer, Rowe, was not even convinced Regret belonged in the race because she was a filly racing against colts. The filly's jockey, Joe Notter, took it upon himself to try to persuade Whitney to leave Regret in the race. Notter made his case to Whitney when the owner stepped off the train. "When H. P. Whitney arrived in Louisville I asked him to run her," Notter recalled. "I told him I didn't think she would have any trouble winning." He persuaded Whitney to keep Regret in the race. After she reached the finish ahead of fifteen males, Whitney entered the winner's circle and exclaimed, "Isn't she the prettiest filly you ever saw?"[15]

Regret was indeed that. The year 1915 was shaping up as the year of the filly. But not for those fillies on Megowan Street. A little more than a month after the Derby, the vice commission filed its long-awaited report with the city government. The commission followed the 1913 grand jury's lead, urging the city to close all bawdy houses by January 1 of the new year.[16] Citizens continued to push for change. The following Sunday, Lexington churches observed a "Purity Sunday." Dean Massie delivered a sermon at Christ Church in which he elaborated on the vice commission's work.

Six months after Regret's historic win at the Kentucky Derby, the Megowan Street houses remained open despite their uncertain future. The Fayette Grand Jury of November raised that old, familiar theme once more: rid the city of prostitution. The jury stated, "There exists no doubt in the minds of the jury that the so-called Red Light district is a menace to the moral and physical well being of the community. . . . It is furthermore true . . . that houses of assignation exist in large numbers in all parts of the city."[17]

At long last, Lexington's city government acted. In November 1915, a pair of antivice ordinances came before the municipal council. They immediately became known as the Twin Vice Ordinances. On the day the ordinances came up for a vote, the council chambers overflowed with spectators. Lawyers, physicians, ministers, coffeehouse owners, and a half-dozen women filled the municipal hall. An offshoot of the vice commission, known as the Committee of Fifteen, had drafted the Twin Vice Ordinances. The committee's legal council, John T. Shelby, spoke eloquently prior to the voting to describe the historic moment at hand. "Let's pass these ordinances and make Lexington a decent place in which to live," Shelby said, his voice ringing through the municipal hall. "A decent place in which fathers and mothers can bring up their children and to which parents in other towns of the country can send their boys and girls to be educated. We can't possibly make things worse, and we may make them a great deal better. These ordinances should be a most efficacious weapon in the hands of the police for law enforcement."[18]

The first of the twin ordinances defined the offense of prostitution and stated the penalties. The second ordinance amended the city's vagrancy law and provided penalties for persons found guilty. The second ordinance also made it clear that any persons caught hanging about the red-light district—visiting men as well as the women who lived there—were to be charged.[19]

City authorities planned to begin enforcing the twin ordinances four days later, on a Monday. But what would this mean for the women on the Hill? Would they take the Twin Vice Ordinances seriously? Where would they go if their neighborhood were shut down? It turned out the women of the Hill did have a place to go. Reformers had come a long way since early in their mission to close the red-light district, when they had not considered the consequences for the madams and their prostitutes. Now they had the future planned for these women: they would open the doors for prostitutes at the House of Mercy on Fourth Street (later the Florence Crittenton Home). Dean Massie expressed doubt that many prostitutes would take advantage of this offer. The majority would simply move on, he told the newspaper, to other cities where vice was winked at.[20]

As the first week in December approached, Lexington stood at the threshold of a new era. The annual tobacco market opened December 1, bringing considerable money into the city. Some among the buyers, sellers, and auctioneers drawn to Lexington during this time would experience a shocking surprise when they discovered their favorite dens of iniquity closed.[21]

The women of the district seemed to be making no effort to resist the new ordinances. One enterprising reporter interviewed a woman of the Hill who spoke fiercely against the hypocrisy she saw in the citizenry. "So help me God," she exclaimed, "I have saved more young girls from a life of shame than all the churches in Lexington." The woman told about befriending a young girl who was innocent of the way of life so familiar to residents of Megowan Street, Dewees (now officially mis-spelled with an "e" at the end of the name), and Wilson streets.

At 3:30 o'clock one morning a young girl came to me and wanted to board here. I never have taken a girl who has not boarded previously. I asked her into my parlor and questioned her.

She said she was sick and hungry and tired. I asked her if she had been seduced and she avowed her virtue. I asked her if she knew the meaning of the word and she said she did. And then I gave her advice. "Go home," I told her, "go jump in the reservoir; go shoot yourself, but never enter here."

I told her to go back home, but first I fed her and put her to bed, unharmed, and before the morning broke and peer-ing eyes could see the house from which she came, I gave her money and sent her to the hospital to be cared for.[22]

As the new week began, many women of the Hill were packing their trunks, preparing to leave Lexington. One madam said she would return home to West Virginia and retire. Another said her house had plummeted in value and would be worth only half the $20,000 she had paid for it. A reporter described this house as a large gray brick on the corner of Wilson and Megowan streets. Quite likely this was Belle's house. The madam said she had contributed handsomely to the econ-omy, spending $10,000 annually on her girls and her house. Did that amount include the stores of wine and beer and hard liquor that she purchased from Lexington merchants? Liquor merchants were going to take a heavy hit when the district closed.[23]

But not all the brothel keepers were ready to shut down so soon after the ordinances passed. They pleaded with the city for more time to close out their business affairs. City authorities relented. A new plan would delay shutting down the brothels until a week before Christ-mas. There would be no more Christmases like that morning when John Jacob Niles sang carols in Belle's house. Nor would there be another Christmas on the Hill like the one when a local banker dressed as Santa Claus and handed out presents to Belle's whores.[24]

At midnight on December 22, 1915, Lexington's red-light district passed into history. The few stragglers who ventured up on the Hill found only a ghost town. The lights were off and the houses dark. The quiet was eerie. Six extra police officers assigned to patrol the district when the twin ordinances took effect remarked on the silence. The quiet streets seemed so unreal, as though a thief had slipped in and stolen all the honky-tonk noise. Signs on many of the houses read "Private Residence."[25]

In January 1916, merchants sent wagons to collect the furniture and paraphernalia they had rented to the brothels. The wagon men loaded their cargoes, turned their horses back toward Main Street, and settled in for the ride. Merchants would miss the income, just as the liquor dealers, the grocery stores, and many other operations ancillary to commercial vice would miss the money they made from business in this neighborhood. The electric and telephone companies would also see their receipts decline with the closing of the brothels. These utility companies reported they had removed many meters and telephones during the preceding week.

There was no sign of Belle. Never one to fight city hall, she had closed her doors, like every other madam in the district. Perhaps she watched the men loading the wagons, parting her curtains ever so slightly to glimpse the horses turning back toward downtown. The sad little wagon procession made its way down Main Street. The following morning's account in the *Lexington Herald* observed the passing of an era: "Yesterday a long stream of drays, bearing electric pianos, music boxes and other mechanical instruments streamed through Main Street, in an almost continuous parade from the former restricted district to the various stores from whom they had been leased."[26] The remains of the era, these instruments of fun and frolic, were now relics.

A few houses on the Hill did reopen, Belle's among them. But Megowan Street was not the same and never would be. The district reemerged as a faint ghost of itself, with these few houses operating in open violation of the Twin Vice Ordinances. For the next two years, Belle ran a scaled-down version of her business, carefully avoiding public attention.

In 1917, Belle's problems were compounded. Billy Mabon died. He had suffered from a chronic kidney inflammation called Bright's disease. His death came on February 16, 1917, and his body was taken to the home of his sister, Alice Morgan, at 408 West Third Street. The pastor of Centenary Methodist Church was to conduct services at the Morgan house. After this, Mabon's body would be taken to Cincinnati for cremation.[27]

On the evening before the services, after all the other visitors had departed, Belle Brezing rang the bell at the Morgan house. Mrs. Morgan admitted her. She permitted Belle to remain alone in the room with Mabon's body, and Belle remained there for some time. Belle did not attend the services the following day. She had lost Grannan. She had lost the Singerlys. And now she had lost her true love, Billy Mabon. She returned alone to the only life she knew on Megowan Street.

When Lexington residents later learned that Belle and a few other brothels, including Blanche Patterson's, had reopened, they were shocked. They thought they had shut down prostitution on Megowan Street. A few more bawdy houses operated nearby on Wilson and Short streets. The citizenry learned this after the U.S. Army training camp commissioner Raymond B. Fosdick dispatched undercover agents to Lexington upon the opening of an army training installation, Camp Stanley. The United States had entered World War I in 1917, and wartime brought a renewed impetus to the social reform movement. When young men enlisted and went off to training camps in faraway places, their parents worried about the temptations their sons might encounter. They pressured cities throughout the country to eliminate any form of vice that might be operating near the camps. Saloons also came under the purview of this renewed reform wave. Fosdick initiated his investigation of Lexington at the urging of Lexington mayor James C. Rogers and George R. Hunt, a longtime reformer. Fosdick informed the mayor that intolerable conditions existed in his city.[28]

One reason these whorehouses had been able to reopen despite the Twin Vice Ordinances was that police did not enforce the ordinances. A grand jury in 1917 noted, "With few exceptions, the police and detective department have given us very little assistance." Fosdick's detectives therefore uncovered disturbing scenarios on the Hill. Belle was running an operation with six prostitutes who "dressed in fancy gowns," just as they always had at Belle's upscale resort. She continued to charge her regulars a $5 fee for a prostitute. She sold Moerlein's beer. But though soldiers roamed the streets of the district, Belle would not admit them to her house.[29]

Blanche Patterson's $2 house did admit soldiers. Patterson kept five prostitutes, who apparently remained quite busy. The detectives discovered nineteen soldiers inside the Patterson resort and eight more soldiers, "ossified drunk," on the stoop of the house, waiting to get inside.[30]

Altogether, the investigators counted 167 soldiers on Megowan, Wilson, and East Short streets. The military patrol was in the neighborhood, but it was not even trying to round up the enlisted men. More to the amazement of investigators, some of the madams informed them they had been warned to be careful because a grand jury was in session. As had always happened in Lexington, municipal insiders were protecting the madams by warning them to lie low.[31]

In the furor that followed at city hall, Police Chief Reagan complained that others had usurped his management of the police department. He resigned. Once more, the brothels were forced to close. This time, when Belle shut down her operation, she closed it for good. She was now fifty-seven years old and, at long last, ready to retire from her life's work.

chapter ELEVEN

The Passing of a Legend

From the time Belle closed her business in 1917 until her death in 1940, Lexington saw little of her. She lived like a recluse inside her mansion. Her only company seemed to be her longtime housekeeper, Pearl Hughes, and a few domestic workers.

The great Man o'War returned home to Lexington in 1921, just as Belle was adjusting to retirement. She would have read about the champion's homecoming because she always read the newspapers. She had subscribed to the *Morning Transcript* in the 1880s when it was Lexington's main source of news, and she remained well read throughout her life.[1] After her retirement, people occasionally glimpsed her reading near a window in the late afternoons. Like everyone else in Lexington, she read about Man o'War retiring from his stellar racing career.

Born and raised at August Belmont II's Nursery Stud on the Georgetown Road, Man o'War had raced in the East but not in Kentucky. Not until the end of the horse's career did he set foot on a local racetrack. On January 28, 1921, Man o'War took his final public gallop in a farewell appearance at the Kentucky Association course. "Down he came," the sports columnist Joe Palmer wrote, "a great red chestnut with a copper mane and a high head, flying the black and yellow silks of Samuel D. Riddle. This was Man o'War, leaving the racetracks forever."[2]

Belle occasionally ventured downtown to conduct her business at the First City National Bank (formerly the Lexington City National Bank) at 518 East Main Street, where an acquaintance, James E. McFarland, was vice president. McFarland and Billy Mabon had worked together at one time, and Belle, knowing McFarland through Mabon, always did her business with him at this bank.

All the while, Belle was getting older and caring less about her aging house. In the early 1920s, after Megowan Street had been renamed Grant Street, Belle's house began to fall apart. Vines ran untended up the side of the house. Weeds grew up in the front yard. A downspout fell on the south side of the house. Belle never bothered to replace it. With the downspout missing, brick on that side of the house began to soak up rainwater. This led to the mortar between the bricks crumbling. Eventually, a large section of the south wall pulled away from the house.[3]

A neighbor informed the city building inspector about the condition of Belle's south wall. Belle, meantime, was considering abandoning the mansion and moving into the house she still owned on Deweese (previously Dewees) Street. She no longer needed the mansion at 153 Grant Street. She thought the move might be less costly than repairing the old brothel.[4]

But Belle was not the kind of neighbor good people wanted to welcome. When African Americans living on Deweese learned of Belle's intentions, they appealed to the city manager, Paul Morton, to stop her from moving into their neighborhood. Morton decided the most diplomatic way to handle this might be to try to talk Belle out of her plan. He sent Margaret Egbert, the policewoman who had grown up with Belle, to persuade Belle not to move. When Egbert walked into the mansion, she saw the decaying remains of the fabled old house. Mirrors still lined the walls in the front portion of the first floor. The famous horn chairs, upholstered in plush red, remained in place in one of the parlors. Moving to the back of the house, Egbert saw that those rooms contained only white enameled beds. In Belle's apartment on the second floor, situated in the front of the house where a bay window faced Grant, Egbert took a look at Belle's bed and remarked, "Big enough for six people to live in." The bedroom suite included a massive dresser, a washstand, and a wardrobe. Egbert said all were made of oak. In the hall outside the bedroom door stood a couch.[5]

Egbert sat down with Belle, and the women had a pleasant visit. Then Egbert segued into her purpose; she suggested to Belle that she would not be able to fit her massive furniture and her numerous books and vases into the small house on Deweese Street. She advised Belle to remain on Grant Street. Belle agreed to change her plans. She repaired the mansion, spending $2,500 to fix the decaying south wall.[6]

Pearl Hughes died on August 29, 1926, after suffering from ovarian cancer. Belle thought the moonshine Pearl drank was a contributing factor, remarking to Pink Thomas that the "shine" killed Pearl. Belle provided Pearl with a burial place in the lot at Calvary Cemetery that Belle had purchased in 1886.[7] Belle had lost another close friend. She hired a new housekeeper, Emma Parker, to replace Pearl.

Although the community saw little of Belle throughout the 1920s and 1930s, the people did not forget her. Her notoriety grew into legend with the passing years. College boys took their dates "cruising" on Grant, pointing out Belle's house. Fraternities sent their young initiates to Grant Street to draw floor plans of the former brothels. Blanche Patterson allowed these initiates to measure the rooms on her first floor.[8]

Sometime during the twentieth century, the gay community in Lexington began to develop an oral tradition embracing Belle as an adopted favorite. This might have grown partly out of James Herndon's practice of sitting with Belle when she was ill, a frequent practice, no doubt due to her morphine habit. Herndon, aka Sweet Evening Breeze, was an orderly at Good Samaritan Hospital and well known throughout the city. He claimed to have taken his drag name partly from Belle's name. "All the old queens [of the 1960s and 1970s] on the north side loved Belle," said Lexington artist Bob Morgan. "She was powerful and a sexual outlaw. She had style and taste. They would all brag about the furniture they took from Belle's. A lot of these queens went to her house." Possibly, the gay community might also have recognized Belle as one of its own. Her suicide pact with another young woman never was fully explained. Had the two been lovers? Morgan said this was not beyond possibility.[9]

In 1933, the Kentucky Association racecourse closed its doors for the final time. The grandstand, the separate ladies' pavilion, the clubhouse, and the betting area and barns would soon be demolished. A new racecourse, Keeneland, opened three years later out in the country on Versailles Road. Keeneland salvaged the seats from the Kentucky Association track; whichever seats Belle and her prostitutes had occupied when watching races at the old track went with the lot to Keeneland.

Belle maintained her secluded life. The only people known to have spent time with her were the Book Thieves, who visited in the late 1930s. By that time, Belle was experiencing increasing pain. Nevitt, her longtime physician, diagnosed ovarian cancer and increased the amount of her morphine dose. By 1940, Belle, now eighty years old, began to decline rapidly. She was unable to get out of bed. Nevitt came to the house several times a day to administer morphine. Parker, the house-keeper, transitioned into Belle's caregiver. Nevitt and Parker moved Belle from her upstairs apartment to a room on the first floor. Nevitt suggested that Belle go to a hospital, but she refused. She wished to die at home.[10]

On August 10, 1940, Belle slipped into a coma. The end lay near. Nevitt telephoned St. Peter Church and asked that a priest come to the house to administer the last rites of the Catholic Church. The pastor, the Reverend Joseph P. Klein, administered the sacrament. Nevitt remained with Belle throughout that night. At 4:30 the next morning, August 11, he pronounced Belle dead.[11]

Belle had given power of attorney to McFarland, her banker, and told him she wanted the Baker Funeral Home to bury her. McFarland's instructions to the funeral home were to bury Belle as quickly as pos-sible. On Monday morning, men at Calvary Cemetery began digging Belle's grave in section O, lot 6. McFarland's intention was to have Belle in the ground before the newspapers learned of her death. In fact, no story appeared in the *Lexington Herald* on Monday morning. Father Klein conducted a brief graveside service. Belle was lowered into her grave, next to her mother's and the marker Belle had erected in her honor, inscribed, "Blessed Be the Pure in Heart." Over the years, Belle had permitted others to be buried in her plot: Pearl Hughes, of course, as well as Rebecca Hall (buried in 1887), Sarah Denny (1929), and Sim-mie C. Culton (1938). Skeets Meadors identified Culton as "a police court character," adding, "People said he was the son of a well-known Lexington whore, 'Big Tit Lil.'"[12]

Rodgers Baker was in his twenties and working at the funeral home when he served as a pallbearer for Belle. Others were C. A. Baker, Rodgers's grandfather; Fred Baker, his father; and John Anglin, an employee of the funeral home. Rodgers Baker said no more than three or four people attended the graveside service. He recalled that one was an African American whom he understood had worked for Belle. Two or three white women who had worked in Belle's house in previous years attended. Belle's funeral expenses totaled $350.[13]

Several hours after the burial, the *Lexington Leader* was the first to inform Lexington residents of Belle's death. A brief notice appeared under a headline with Belle's name misspelled: "Bell Breazing Dead." The notice read, "Funeral services and burial were to be held at 2 o'clock this afternoon for Bell Breazing, who died at 4:30 o'clock Sunday morning at her home at Wilson Street and North Eastern Avenue. She is survived by one daughter, Daisy Kenney, of Dearborn, Mich."[14]

The big story about "Lexington's prototype of the Belle Watling of 'Gone With the Wind'" appeared the following morning, Tuesday, August 13, in the *Lexington Herald*. It began, "Death has closed another chapter of Lexington's history—a story which historians hesitated to write, but unwritten, has been elaborated until it had drifted well nigh into the field of legend." The story does not carry a byline, but the writer was city editor J. R. "Babe" Kimbrough. He took over the story after he rejected a reporter's first version as too vivid. Kimbrough and a photographer, Tom Stone, went to Belle's house. While the photographer took pictures inside and out, Kimbrough interviewed Parker, the maid.[15] Kimbrough wrote of Belle as a "colorful character of the Gay Nineties and early Nineteen Hundreds." His story continued, "Once the operator of one of the largest and most lavish establishments south of the Mason-Dixon line, she had in recent years lived in seclusion in the dimly lit, decaying ruins of her once heavily gilded-and-mirrored 'mansion for men.' Her only companion was a Negro maid." A photograph accompanying Kimbrough's page-one story, appropriately captioned, "A Ghost House on North Eastern Avenue," presented an eerie picture of the ruined house.[16]

Kimbrough described the interior of the house as replete with decay, "fallen plaster and rotting woodwork" everywhere he looked. "The ballroom, with its red walls and mirrored ceiling, was still there. But all that remained of the room's furnishings was a huge mechanical piano standing like a mummified sentinel in one corner of the hall—its keys yellowed by the years and its handsomely carved cabinet lined with dust and cobwebs accumulated through decades of silence." The private parlor "which, according to legend, had been the scene of entertainment of many influential men," appeared intact. Inside Kimbrough glimpsed the much-talked-about red horn chairs. Kimbrough described the entrance hall "with its richly carved stairway leading to the upper-floor apartments." At the rear of the first floor, he discovered the wine room. The old wine racks remained, but all were empty. The doors of huge cupboards stood ajar, their empty shelves covered in soot. Parker told Kimbrough: "Miss Belle had just let things go since she had been sick. I haven't been in some of these rooms in years." Kimbrough concluded, "The house, its furnishings and the dank atmosphere was a silent monument to the gilded era it represented. There was a strange sense of forlornness about it all—like a temple built upon the sands that had been crumpled by the tide of moral righteousness."[17]

By 10:00 Tuesday morning, the *Lexington Herald*'s entire run of nineteen thousand copies had been sold out. Circulation manager Tom Adams said it was the first time he could remember the *Herald* selling out on a weekday. Scalpers saw their opportunity: a single copy of the newspaper went for as much as $1. Public reaction from women readers especially was indignant; many telephoned the newspaper offices objecting to the story. "Is it true that to get on the front page of the *Herald* one must operate a house of ill repute?"[18]

Time magazine's obituary recognized Belle with the highest praise she could have received, noting the passing of the "famed Kentucky bawd" who operated a "plushy, luxuriant salon, famed for its influential patrons and for being the most orderly of disorderly houses."[19]

Belle was barely in the ground before a longtime Lexington resident, Joe Graves, mailed sympathy cards to a number of men, reading, "The family of Belle Breazing acknowledges with grateful appreciation your kind expression of sympathy." These cards were said to have caused many a family fight when they arrived. Years later, Graves owned up to his prank, admitting police chief Bud McCloy told him that "the sympathy cards I mailed out at the time brought so much anguish and humiliation into the homes of our best citizens that I should have been put under lock and key."[20]

On the day of Belle's burial, McFarland hired a man named Bill McCowan to guard the empty house. He also contacted an auctioneer, Sam Downing, to arrange for a public auction of Belle's furniture and personal items. Nine days after Belle's funeral, an advertisement for the auction appeared in the *Lexington Leader,* the date set for August 22 at 10:00 a.m. For sale were the

> entire contents of building including large mirrors; famous horn suite furniture; cut-glass; silver; china; bric-a-brac of all kinds and other furniture.
>
> Also, fifty-one pieces of jewelry consisting of a diamond necklace; diamond solitaire rings; diamond dinner rings; rings made of other precious stones; and other jewelry of gold and stones of many kinds.

Downing had some idea what to expect when he auctioned the items because Fayette County Court had requested three appraisers to tally the value of Belle's jewelry. They placed a value of $600 on a diamond necklace, $500 on a diamond twin Tiffany ring, $250 on another diamond twin Tiffany ring, $400 on a diamond solitaire, and so on for forty-nine items including rings, lockets, watches, and bracelets. Appraisers valued her furniture at only $350.[21]

On auction day, people began lining up at the door several hours ahead of the start time. Around 9:00, police had to rope off Eastern Avenue to traffic because of the size of the crowd. By the time the auction began, the crowd not only filled the street in front of Belle's house but spread up and down Eastern Avenue and around the corner onto Wilson Street. African Americans who had begun moving back into the neighborhood after the brothels shut down sold Coca-Cola from their porches. Many women were part of the curious crowd, and many women purchased Belle's possessions, despite objections less than a month earlier to the *Lexington Herald's* story about Belle.[22]

So many people attended the auction that Downing was forced to continue the sale for two more days. On the third day, he auctioned the furniture. None other than Clara Sayre purchased Belle's bedroom suite, paying $1,600. At nightfall, Downing locked the empty house. All of Belle's personal items had been sold and taken away. Vandals wasted no time; they began smashing windows the day after the auction.[23]

Daisy May was now sixty-five years old. Probate court for Wayne County, Michigan, appointed a man named Floyd Frye as her guardian. As part of this process, the court heard from several people who offered evaluations of Daisy May's condition. The chief of staff at St. Joseph's Retreat, physician Russell T. Costello, stated, "Daisy Kenney is feeble-minded and hopelessly incurable." Frye repeated this assessment. Another physician, Edward M. Mooney, testified, "When asked her age she says she is fourteen and that her mother is twelve." In the evaluation of another physician, Harriet L. Hawkins, Daisy May was "full of notions and strange ideas." Frye summed it up: "She needs care in an institution."[24]

McFarland and Nevitt both submitted depositions to the Michigan court; both said no family member could be found to take care of Daisy May. "My impression is from hearsay that she has two first cousins," Nevitt testified, "but they have not been heard from in nine or ten years. We do not know whether they are living or dead. These two cousins are the sons of a deceased sister of Daisy Kenney's mother. My information is that their names are Carl Norton, who used to live on Vine Street, in Cincinnati, Ohio, and worked in a restaurant, and James Barry Norton, who lived in Vancouver, British Columbia, and was an actor. James had a wife and two children." Concluding the matter of Daisy May, the court appointed Frye as the woman's guardian and instructed him to turn over to St. Joseph's Retreat any and all money he received from the estate of Daisy May's mother.[25]

Daisy May did not live long after her mother's death. On August 3, 1948, she was sent from St. Joseph's Retreat to St. Mary's Hospital in Detroit. Two days later, she suffered a broken hip and underwent surgery. She died August 15 at the hospital. Burial took place at St. Hedwig in Dearborn Heights, Michigan, a cemetery in the care of Franciscan monks. Indigents such as Daisy May were buried anonymously. Thompson wrote, "A young man consulted his records and led the way to Section One, Lot One. . . . The monk explained that bodies are buried as they are received; by counting from the first grave, it is possible to locate a particular one. And he indicated the spot where Daisy May is buried."[26]

Next came the sale of Belle's real estate. The Deweese Street property sold to J. Rice Porter on April 21, 1941, for $1,300. George Hoskins bought the mansion on Eastern Avenue for $3,117 on the same day. A real estate agent involved in this transfer said the mansion was in bad repair. Windows were broken. Many fixtures had been removed. The plumbing was old. Thompson wrote, "He estimated it would take four or five thousand dollars to put the house in livable condition."[27]

Not a lot of money remained in Belle's estate. Upon her death, she had $124.76 in her checking account. Sam Downing's auction of her effects brought in $5,756.52. She owned thirty-six shares in First National Bank, worth $3,600. She had $126 in dividends from that stock. These assets totaled $9,607.28.[28]

Nolan Carter, the administrator for the estate, produced a list of deductions that revealed how various entities chipped away at Belle's final assets: $730.36 to Carter as administrator, $20 to Victor Bogaert Jr. to appraise the jewelry, $10 to Calvary Cemetery, $80.64 to the *Lexington Herald* and the *Lexington Leader* to advertise the auction, $50 to Katherine Carter to clean and prepare the house for the auction, $580.56 to Downing for his auctioneer's commission, $219 to Nevitt, and so on. Floyd Frye received $5,479.83 to be used for Daisy May's care, an amount that included the thirty-six bank shares. St. Joseph's Retreat received $1,567.50 for an unpaid bill.[29]

Belle's former mansion for men took on a new purpose as a boarding house during World War II. An African American woman, Flora Hudson, rented out rooms in this house she called the Hudson Hotel. She contracted with the U.S. Army to house African American soldiers coming through Lexington, because segregation barred these men from staying in most city hotels. Hudson also rented to people discharged from the old narcotics hospital on Leestown Road. People called Mrs. Hudson "Mama Flora." She rented the house until the mid-1960s, when the owners converted the building to thirteen apartments, renaming the building the Floral Apartments.[30]

On December 12, 1973, the house caught fire. Firefighters from eight units responded. The American Red Cross served coffee and sandwiches at the site to firefighters and police. A woman trapped in her third-floor apartment was rescued and transported to Good Samaritan Hospital, where she later died. The fire gutted several apartments and the roof and attic. Firefighters determined that a seven-year-old boy had started the fire; he admitted to squirting lighter fluid over some furnishings in an apartment and on an open-flame gas room heater. The boy escaped the flames by jumping from his second-floor window onto the top of a car parked below.[31]

Not all thought the heavily damaged building beyond repair. Joe Graves of Lexington and another local businessman, Bill Rice, contacted the building's owner, E. B. Sparks, and told him they had a great idea for turning the house into a restaurant. But the restaurant never materialized. Sparks prepared to go ahead with demolition and set up an auction to sell off the remaining architectural features in the old house. A rather poetic advertisement for this auction read:

> Little is left of the elegance that had paid host to the famous and infamous of a bygone era. Wallpaper in a cherub pattern hangs water soaked from the ceiling, in a room that once echoed to the call of "ladies to the parlor." The wood of a parquet floor, loosed by fire hoses, lie like children's blocks scattered in an empty hall. Mantel mirrors that once reflected candlelight, now look out on the decay of another life.
>
> True, little is left, but who of you can dream a "back bar" from an old mantel, or a use for old gold molding in the parlor ceiling, a curio box or desk ornament from floor blocks; who will bid on the iron mantel from Miss Annie's room for a conversation piece in a den or recreation room; start the bidding on a stained glass window that illuminated the stairs where satin mustled [sic] skirts led the way to the second floor; who can use a gingerbread stairway that could tell a thousand tales? How about bricks for a fireplace or a garden wall? What can be made of old door facings or the inside shutters that separated "fallen flowers" from the prime [sic] Victorian world outside?
>
> If you can't stand quietly, in the midst of clutter, and hear soft voices, the tinkle of Champagne glasses, or the wail of a down hearted frail floating back over the years, don't bother to come. It's a spooky old house, and we have nothing to sell but nostalgia.

Everything that could be removed was sold: mantels, doors, and one entire room, purchased by a man from Tennessee who reportedly planned to install it as a den in the home of a country singer. After bulldozers leveled the house, even the bricks were sold as souvenirs.[32]

Thompson related a tale about the final auction:

> On the day of the auction, one of the first men to arrive said
> that he had heard one of Belle's old girls was coming to the
> sale. Shortly afterwards, a chauffeur-driven limousine pulled
> up in front of the house and two elderly ladies, very tastefully
> dressed, were helped from the car by the driver. Each carried
> a gold-headed cane.
>
> On entering the house, they went from room to room,
> looking at each wall, ceiling, floor, and doorway. . . . On the
> second floor, they went from room to room. Occasionally, one
> would point with her cane. The rooms were empty. There was
> nothing to point to unless to indicate where some piece of
> furniture had stood or where some event had occurred. After
> inspecting the entire second floor, they returned to the auto-
> mobile and left.[33]

True or not, this tale demonstrates how even upon demolition of the
house, Belle and her brothel loomed large in the imagination.

One other testament to Belle's special place in the community's
imagination was the matter of her bed, reportedly given or sold to her by
the gambler Riley Grannan. After Clara Sayre, Flora Hudson became
the bed's next owner. According to Thompson, Hudson turned down
many offers to sell the bed, including a former governor's bid of $7,000.
When she died in May 1987, her estate deemed that the bed go up for
auction. The successful bidder was Kirtley B. Amos, an attorney in Lexington, who bought the bed for $12,600 (plus sales tax, which brought
the total to $13,230).[34]

Ernest Featherstone was the last of Belle's close friends to die, on
July 22, 1945, in Bourbon County. The final link to the old brothel was
gone.

Even Belle might have trouble finding the way to the site of her old
whorehouse now. A family home occupies the property where Belle's
mansion once stood. Gone is every physical reminder that this was
the site of the Brezing mansion for men. Memory of Belle remains
very much alive, however, and occupies an exotic place in the history
of Lexington and the surrounding horse country. Periodically, residents

of this city have celebrated Belle by naming racehorses for her. They have staged memorial events such as the Belle Brezing Bed Race for two-legged runners and a horse race named for her at the Red Mile. The trotting track inaugurated that race in 1983 with a "Belle Brezing Look-Alike" contest and a $500 prize. (Both the pacing race and the human one have since been discontinued.)[35]

So listen closely if you walk down Main Street beside Thoroughbred Park and look up the Hill on Eastern Avenue early in the evening. You might hear in your imagination the tinkling of mechanical pianos spilling forth from the parlors of the brothels. You might hear the high notes of female laughter commingled with the deeper voices of many men. You might even hear Belle Brezing's voice, welcoming gentlemen callers to her house.

Epilogue

For generations, fans of the novel and movie *Gone with the Wind* have speculated about whether Margaret Mitchell modeled her character Belle Watling after Belle Brezing. Mitchell denied this to her death in 1949, as did her husband, John Marsh. But few people believed these denials. In her biography of Margaret Mitchell, Marianne Walker speculated that a connection had to exist because too many coincidences linked the two Belles. Belle Brezing's hair was red; so was Belle Watling's. The novel's descriptions of Belle Watling's house match the glimpses we have of Belle Brezing's mansion. Both madams accepted as clients only men of financial means. Both women attempted to give large donations to charitable institutions, only to be rebuffed because of their profession.[1]

Marsh worked the police beat for the *Lexington Leader* while attending the University of Kentucky during the 1910s (some years before his marriage to Mitchell), fueling further speculation that Belle Watling was indeed modeled on the notorious Belle Brezing. Mitchell would not have known how to describe the inside of a brothel, as Walker wrote. But Marsh would have. Belle Brezing's kitchen was always open to police officers and reporters who covered the police beat. "In exchange for her [Belle's] culinary offerings," according to Walker, "she could depend on the policemen to restore order in case there were fights, or to dispatch drunks, and she could count on the newspapermen to keep silent about certain reports and the names of certain clients." Walker learned in an interview with John Marsh's sister-in-law, Francesca Marsh, that John spent many nights in Belle's kitchen with a police officer, enjoying a fine meal and hearing colorful stories about the demimonde of the red-light district on the Hill. Francesca Marsh told Walker that Marsh related these stories to his brothers and later to his wife.[2]

Why did Mitchell deny the Belle connection? When she composed her manuscript, she apparently thought the resemblance between Belle Watling and Belle Brezing was unimportant because she wrote the manuscript for herself, not for publication. Walker and another Mitchell biographer, Anne Edwards, agree that Mitchell, a journalist, wrote fiction only for her own amusement. The unexpected happened when Macmillan accepted the manuscript for publication in 1936 and it became wildly popular, Walker wrote. Mitchell won the Pulitzer Prize for her novel, and more than 30 million copies are in print worldwide. The 1939 film adaptation was likewise a huge popular success. Mitchell and Marsh had envisioned none of this; they believed that sales would number only a few thousand, with most books going to relatives or to libraries in Georgia. "She was not concerned about the Watling character," according to Walker, "because Lexington, Kentucky, was many miles away from Atlanta, where people had never heard of Belle Brezing or, even if they had, they would not know any details of her life." The surprising success of *Gone with the Wind* might have prompted Mitchell and Marsh to fear that Belle Brezing would sue them, speculated Lexington newsman Joe Jordan. Mitchell was still denying Belle Watling's similarity to the real Belle when she and Marsh visited Lexington in November 1940, three months after Belle Brezing's death.[3]

Thompson never believed these denials. He stated quite clearly in his biography of Belle Brezing: "A comparison of the life of Belle Brezing and the fictional character of Belle Watling makes it obvious that John Marsh had told his wife tales of Brezing and that Margaret Mitchell drew on these to create Belle Watling."[4] There seems little doubt that Lexington's most notorious brothel keeper was given new life in *Gone with the Wind*. But in a sense it hardly matters: Belle's real-life story in old Lexington is as fascinating as any fiction.

Acknowledgments

The author would like to thank the following people and organizations for their assistance: Richard Stone and his private library for Standard-bred horses in Sadieville, Kentucky; the Keeneland Association Library; the Kentucky Room of the Lexington Public Library; Special Collections and Archives of the University of Kentucky; Special Collections of Transylvania University Library; Kentucky Department for Libraries; and the Harness Racing Museum and Hall of Fame.

Notes

Preface

1. Clark, *My Century in History*, 343.

1. The Elegant Miss Belle

1. "Nomad in the Blue Grass Country—The Famous Breeding Studs," *Turf, Field and Farm*, December 1, 1871, 337. Custer's articles on horse racing for *Turf, Field and Farm* also have been collected in Dippie, *Nomad*.

2. 1890 Fayette County Tax Assessment Book.

3. Goodloe G. Clay to Isaac Murphy, Fayette County Deed Book 68, 453, November 5, 1883; Isaac and Lucy Murphy to Gustave Luigart, Fayette County Deed Book 103, 348, July 12, 1894. These deeds concern Murphy's purchase and sale of his Megowan Street property.

4. Thompson, *Madam Belle Brezing*, 62, 76.

5. "Ed Corrigan's Crime," *Chicago Daily Inter Ocean*, November 5, 1887; "Ed Corrigan's Cruelty," *Chicago Daily Inter Ocean*, July 25, 1888; "An Incorrigible Character," *Thoroughbred Record*, May 20, 1981, 2225; "Ed Corrigan Uses His Gun for a Gavel in a Directors' Meeting," *Lexington Morning Herald*, September 22, 1896.

6. "Ed Corrigan Here," *Lexington Morning Herald*, January 25, 1903; "Ed Corrigan, Once Famous on the Turf, Now Carries His Dinner Pail," *Duluth News Tribune*, August 18, 1912.

7. "Train of 114 Trotters to Chicago, Charge of E. L. Featherstone," *Lexington Herald*, January 14, 1903; "Horses for Austria," *Cleveland Leader*, December 1, 1897; "Hoof Beats," *Saginaw Evening News*, July 16, 1898.

8. Ernest Featherstone interview with Skeets Meadors, Thompson Papers, box 41, folder 21.

9. Colonel Phil Chinn interview, February 9, 1956, Thompson Papers, box 41, folder 45.

10. Robertson and Farley, *Hoofprints of the Century*, 69.

2. Civil War and Home War

1. Coleman, *The Squire's Sketches of Lexington*, 49; Sarah Ann's surname is spelled Cocks on her marriage license to George Brezing, December 16, 1861, Thompson Papers, box 40, folder 15.

2. Thompson, *Madam Belle Brezing*, 13–15.

3. Deposition of Thomas Webster, taken at the office of James Mulligan, June 6, 1866, *Sarah Brezing vs. George Brezing*.

4. Deposition of Bettie Coons, taken at the office of James Mulligan, June 6, 1866, *Sarah Brezing vs. George Brezing,*

5. Deposition of James Millburn, taken at the office of James Mulligan, June 6, 1866, *Sarah Brezing vs. George Brezing*. The man's name might have been spelled Milbourne. Handwritten records are conflicting and unclear.

6. Deposition of Hester Brezing, taken at the office of James Mulligan, June 6, 1866, *Sarah Brezing vs. George Brezing*.

7. Lowry and White, *A Century of Speed*, 11; Coleman, *The Squire's Sketches of Lexington*, 10–11.

8. Coleman, *Lexington during the Civil War*, 11.

9. Ibid., 2.

10. Ibid., 3–5.

11. Smith, *Window on the War*, 12.

12. Recollections of George W. Ranck, *Daily Lexington Transcript*, November 14, 1882, quoted in Coleman, *Lexington during the Civil War*, 20.

13. Ramage, *Rebel Raider*, 95; Coleman, *Lexington during the Civil War*, 20–21.

14. Coleman, *Lexington during the Civil War;* see also Ramage, *Rebel Raider*, 103–4.

15. Pratt Diary, quoted in Coleman, *Lexington during the Civil War*, 21–22.

16. Coleman, *Lexington during the Civil War*, 24.

17. Ibid., 24.

18. Ibid., 25–26; Ramage, *Rebel Raider*, 120.

19. Coleman, *Lexington during the Civil War*, 28–32; Ramage, *Rebel Raider*, 124.

20. Smith, *Window on the War*, 38, 44–45.

21. Ibid., 32–33.

22. Crickmore, *Racing Calendars, 1861–1865*, 18.

23. Smith, *Window on the War*, 17, 34, 28.

24. Mackay-Smith, *The Race Horses of America*, 311; Coleman, *Lexington during the Civil War*, 38; Ramage, *Rebel Raider*, 220.

3. A Troubled Youth

1. Skeets Meadors notes, Thompson Papers, box 38, folder 8. Meadors noted: "Miss [Linda] Neville and Mrs. Margaret Egbert . . . remember Belle attended old No. 2 school on West Main St., where the Salvation Army now is." Meadors also wrote that Belle lived near the Jefferson Street end of Main Street. According to Jacob Speyer interview, Thompson Papers, box 41, folder 20, he lived in the same block as Belle when he was a boy and confirmed that Belle went to No. 2 School across the street.

2. Mrs. Florence [Margaret] Egbert interview, Thompson Papers, box 40, folder 4. Egbert said she attended Dudley School at the same time as Belle, that Belle dressed well, and "We kids couldn't understand why our families would not let us have anything to do with her."

3. Deposition of James R. Heatherington, April 7, 1866, *Sarah Brezing vs. George Brezing.*

4. Deposition of John Worth, April 7, 1866, *Sarah Brezing vs. George Brezing.*

5. Ibid.

6. William S. McMeekin and Sallie Brezing, May 18, 1870, Kentucky Marriages, 1785–1979; *Prather's Lexington City Directory for 1875 and 1876,* 157.

7. Thompson, *Madam Belle Brezing,* 17, 22; Belle Brezing 1874 scrapbook, Thompson Papers, box 38, folder 7.

8. Tanner, "Fifty Years Recollections of Lexington and Vicinity," 11.

9. Bolin, *Bossism and Reform in a Southern City,* 20, 13–16.

10. Ibid., 16.

11. *The Commonwealth of Kentucky vs. James E Pepper and William S Barnes,* "Nuisance," Fayette County Indictments, box 13, drawer 110–12, Kentucky Department for Libraries, Frankfort.

12. Tanner, "Fifty Years Recollections of Lexington and Vicinity," 124.

13. Ibid.

14. *Lexington Fire Department Commemorative Book,* 9.

15. Womack, "The Urban Development of Lexington, 1870–1910"; Tanner, "Fifty Years Recollections of Lexington and Vicinity," 7.

16. Skeets Meadors notes, Thompson Papers. Meadors stated that the Mucci house and the Mucci business place lots connected at the rear of each. Meadors also wrote that Neville, who lived at 722 West Main Street, told him in an interview that the Mucci house was not on the northeast corner of Main and Georgetown streets. This house was occupied by another person. Apparently the Mucci residence was the next house facing Main Street.

17. Thompson, *Madam Belle Brezing,* 22.

18. Ibid., 22–23; Skeets Meadors notes, Thompson Papers. Meadors wrote he had long heard from old-timers in Lexington that a man named Mucci had

"ruined" Belle when she was very young. Meadors said Jacob Speyer, who lived in the same block as Belle, had heard the Mucci story.

19. Sparks, *Kentucky's Most Hated Man*, 242–43.

20. On Breckinridge, see Kleber, *The Kentucky Encyclopedia*, 121.

21. Brezing scrapbook, Thompson Papers, box 38, folder 7.

22. Ibid.

23. Ibid.

24. Ibid.

25. Ibid.

26. Thompson, *Madam Belle Brezing*, 28.

27. Ibid., 29–30.

28. *Lexington Daily Press*, September 15, 1875, quoted in ibid., 30.

29. *Lexington Daily Press*, September 24, 1875; Thompson, *Madam Belle Brezing*, 30–31.

30. "A Suicide or a Murder," *Lexington Daily Press*, September 24, 1875.

31. Ibid.

32. Ibid.

33. Ibid.

34. "Post Mortem Affection," *Lexington Leader*, September 25, 1875.

35. Ibid.

36. "Suicide or Murder," *Lexington Daily Press*, September 28, 1875.

37. Ibid.

38. Thompson, *Madam Belle Brezing*, 35.

4. A Businesswoman Whose Business Was Men

1. Walzer and Numbers, *Sickness and Health in America*, 418. John Duffy writes in his chapter in the book that prior to the bacteriological revolution in the late nineteenth century, "epidemic and endemic diseases were as inexplicable and mysterious to man as they had been to his most primitive forebears. . . . In the second half of the 19th century . . . the health records of every city show that tuberculosis, diphtheria, scarlet fever, whooping cough, enteric disorders, measles, smallpox, and even malaria were endemic."

2. *Prather's Lexington City Directory for 1875 and 1876*, 265.

3. Rosenberg, *The Care of Strangers*. Rosenberg notes an antebellum tradition that "ordinarily a home atmosphere and the nursing of family members provided the ideal conditions for restoring health" (21). The poverty stricken might find themselves in an almshouse. The author writes that in the late eighteenth century, Philadelphia Hospital discerned between the deserving and undeserving by requiring "a written testimonial from a 'respectable' person attesting to the moral worth of an applicant before he or she could be admitted to a bed" (19).

4. Duffy writes, "A few empirical discoveries, such as vaccination for small pox, had led to some improvement in conditions of health, but the origin and transmission of diseases were as obscure as ever."

5. "The Fire," *Lexington Daily Press,* May 16, 1876; Tanner, "Fifty Years Recollections of Lexington and Vicinity," 109.

6. "City Council: All Proper Precaution Taken to Prevent the Spread of Small-Pox," Moses Kaufman Papers, scrapbook 3, 11–33.

7. A monument Belle commissioned in honor of her mother stated Sarah was born May 5, 1836, and died May 19, 1876.

8. "Phoenix Hotel, Lexington, Ky.," *Lexington Daily Press,* May 13, 1876; "Lexington," *Spirit of the Times,* May 24, 1879, 380; "The Kentucky Association," *Thoroughbred Record,* October 27, 1900, 197.

9. "The Fire."

10. "The Turf," *Lexington Daily Press,* May 16, 1876; "Dispatches Every Day," *Lexington Daily Press,* May 16, 1876.

11. Weather data provided by the Midwestern Regional Climate Center, Champaign, Ill., show .50 inches of rain fell in Lexington May 17; .45 inches on May 18; and .23 inches on May 19. Thompson, *Madam Belle Brezing,* 35.

12. Birds Eye View of Lexington, KY, 1871, shows railroad tracks crossing over the top of that point where Leestown Pike joined West Main Street. For slope gradient at this point, see Topographical Map, Lexington West, KY, 1965.

13. Blanche Patterson interview, noted in "Jennie Hill's Place," Thompson Papers, box 40, folder 2. Patterson said Belle told her that while she was burying her mother, the landlord had thrown the Brezing possessions out on the sidewalk and padlocked the door.

14. Tandy Hughes interview, Thompson Papers, box 40, folder 4.

15. Egbert interview. She is mistakenly identified as Florence Egbert.

16. Tanner, "Fifty Years Recollections of Lexington and Vicinity," 8; "A Short Life and a Hard One: How Car Horses are Bought, Broken, Patched up and Retired," *Lexington Daily Press,* January 9, 1889.

17. Tanner, "Fifty Years Recollections of Lexington and Vicinity," 8.

18. Ibid., 7, 11; Womack, "The Urban Development of Lexington, 1870–1910."

19. "The Town Cows," *Lexington Daily Transcript,* June 25, 1879; notes of a city council meeting believed to have been held in 1879, Kaufman Papers, box 3; Pryor, *Doctor Pryor,* 85; Womack, "The Urban Development of Lexington, 1870–1910"; "Their First Meeting," *Lexington Leader,* May 2, 1890, 3.

20. *Lexington Leader,* January 6, 1890, 1.

21. Hollingsworth, *Lexington,* 125; "Stanton Shows His Ears," written for the *Cincinnati Post,* reprinted in *Kentucky Leader,* October 3, 1890, 3.

22. Tanner, "Fifty Years Recollections of Lexington and Vicinity," 8.

23. Pryor, *Doctor Pryor,* 105.

24. R. C. Hellrigle & Co., *Lexington City Directory,* 26.

25. *Lexington Daily Press,* July 26, 1879; "Suicidal," *Canton Daily Repository,* July 26, 1879, 1.

26. *Lexington Daily Press,* July 26, 1879.

27. *Lexington Daily Press,* July 25, 1879.

28. *Lexington Daily Press,* July 26, 1879.

29. Musto, *The American Disease.*

30. "A Bounding Human Ball," *Lexington Daily Press,* June 29, 1879.

31. Ibid.

32. Ibid.

33. Thompson, *Madam Belle Brezing,* 38; *Williams' Lexington City Directory for 1881–82,* 95. The directory lists Jennie Hill as residing at the southeast corner of Main and Merino.

34. The U.S. Census for 1880 lists Jennie Hill as age thirty-three at the time of enumeration, June 2, 1880. The census year began June 1, 1879, and ended May 31, 1880. See also *Williams' Lexington City Directory for 1881–82,* 36, which lists "Belle Breesing" boarding at the southeast corner of Main and Merino.

35. "The Kentucky Association," *Thoroughbred Record,* August 25, 1900.

36. "The Kentucky Association," *Thoroughbred Record,* August 18, 1900, September 1, 1900; "Lexington Spring Meeting," *Spirit of the Times,* May 28, 1870, 226.

37. Womack, "The Urban Development of Lexington, 1870–1910," 9–10; "The Kentucky Association," *Thoroughbred Record,* August 4, 1900.

38. "The Kentucky Association," *Thoroughbred Record,* July 28, 1900.

39. "The Turf in America," *Spirit of the Times,* December 24, 1870, 296.

40. Lowry and White, *A Century of Speed,* 10; *Lexington Daily Transcript,* June 26, 1879; "Among the Blue-Grass Trotters," *Harper's New Monthly Magazine,* October 1883, 716; "For Sale," *American Citizen,* November 13, 1875; Lowry and White, *A Century of Speed,* 11, 18.

5. Networks of Power

1. Hollingsworth, *The Great Ones,* 145; Robertson, *The History of Thoroughbred Racing in America.*

2. Belle Brezing to Charles F. Brower Jr. and Joseph M. Scott, trading under the firm name of Brower & Scott, July 8, 1881, Fayette County Mortgage Book 7, 196; Thompson, *Madam Belle Brezing,* 45; Angie Muhs, "Transy Plan for Women's Field Preserves Historic Brothel," *Lexington Herald-Leader,* March 10, 1995.

3. Belle Brezing to Sutton & Son, July 11, 1881, Fayette County Mortgage Book 7, 218.

4. "The Phoenix Hotel," *Lexington Transcript,* October 20, 1889.

5. "Phoenix Hotel," in Kleber, *The Kentucky Encyclopedia,* 719–20. On Custer, see Wall, *How Kentucky Became Southern,* 78–89.

6. Kleber, *The Kentucky Encyclopedia,* 719–20.

7. Sayers, *Lexington Club.*

8. Ibid.

9. Gano Lee interview, July 8, 1982, Thompson Papers, box 41, folder 5; Thompson, *Madam Belle Brezing,* 84.

10. Sayers, *Lexington Club.*

11. Ibid.; Clara Sayre interview with Joe Jordan, August 1, 1941, Thompson Papers, box 40, folder 1; John Coyne interview, Thompson Papers, box 40, folder 4.

12. Sayers, *Lexington Club.*

13. Kaufman Papers, box 3, scrapbook 2.

14. Ranck, *A Review of Lexington,* 106.

15. "A College for Horses," *Clark's Horse Review,* February 1, 1889, 13.

16. Kaufman Papers, box 3, scrapbook 1, 113–14, 121.

17. Ibid., box 3, scrapbook 1, 127.

18. "Hung in Effigy," *Lexington Transcript,* February 28, 1881, located in Kaufman Papers, box 3, scrapbook 1, 130.

19. Belle Brezing to Brower & Scott, July 8, 1881, Fayette County Mortgage Book 7, 196. Marginal notation states the loan was satisfied December 30, 1881; Belle Brezing to Sutton & Son, July 11, 1881, Fayette County Mortgage Book 7, 218; Belle Brezing to Sutton & Son, March 25, 1882, Fayette County Mortgage Book 8, 187.

20. Alice Jackson and husband to Belle Brezing, July 18, 1883, Fayette County Deed Book 68, 189; Thompson collection, no. 40, 5. In his notes, Thompson stated this address was the third house south of Fourth Street.

21. Luke P. Blackburn, governor of the Commonwealth of Kentucky, February 7, 1883, original pardon in Thompson Papers, box 39, folder 4.

22. Margaret Egbert interview with Burton Milward, March 28, 1940, Thompson Papers, box 40, folder 5.

23. Typed notes, Thompson Papers, box 40, folder 4.

24. Belle Brezing to William and J. R. Williamson, December 17, 1883, Fayette County Mortgage Book 10, 82; Belle Brezing to Asa Dodge, March 18, 1885, Fayette County Mortgage Book 11, 451; Belle Brezing to Williamson & Brother, May 8, 1886, Fayette County Mortgage Book 12, 128; Belle Brezing to Asa Dodge, July 23, 1886, Fayette County Mortgage Book 13, 454; Belle Brezing to Scott & Skillman, March 18, 1886, Fayette County Mortgage Book 12, 81.

25. W. L. Taylor to Belle Brezing, October 25, 1886, Fayette County Deed

Book 76, 155; P. & C. Crostwait to Belle Brezing, November 22, 1888, Fayette County Deed Book 82, 2.

26. *Commonwealth of Kentucky v. Belle Brezing,* December 12, 1882.

27. C. J. Bronston to Gov. S. B. Buckner, January 11, 1888; J. C. Rogers to Gov. S. B. Buckner, December 8, 1890; S. G. Sharp to Governor S. B. Buckner, January 13, 1888; E. L. Hutchinson to Hon. S. B. Buckner, December 8, 1890. All letters contained in Thompson Papers, box 40, folder 20.

28. *Commonwealth of Kentucky v. Belle Brezing,* November 26, 1866.

29. *Commonwealth of Kentucky v. James Cox,* November 29, 1886.

30. Sparks, *Kentucky's Most Hated Man,* 45, 47, 144.

31. Ibid., 190.

32. Ibid., 231.

33. Ibid., 154–55; "The Fairlawn Sale," *Kentucky Stock Farm,* October 17, 1889, 12–13.

34. Thompson, *Madam Belle Brezing,* 49, 46; Hughes interview.

35. Belle Brezing Account Book, 1882–883, Thompson Papers, box 40, folder 4.

36. Ibid., 3, 219, 223; Belle Brezing Account Book, n.d., Thompson Papers, box 38, folder 2.

37. "Bal de Demi-monde," *Morning Lexington Transcript,* May 12, 1883; Belle Brezing Account Book, 1887, box 38, folder 2, 52.

38. Pink Thomas interview with Skeets Meadors, Thompson Papers, box 41, folder 6; Thompson, *Madam Belle Brezing,* 70. A book titled *Lucille* by Owen Meredith that Mabon presented to Belle was inscribed, "From Will to Kitten, March 4, 1888," Thompson Papers, box 38, folder 9.

39. *Prather's Lexington City Directory for 1875 and 1876,* 158; R. C. Hellrigle & Co., *Lexington City Directory,* 74; *Williams' Lexington City Directory,* 129; *Townsend and Company's Lexington Directory for 1883–1884,* 125; *City Directory of Lexington, Kentucky, 1887; City Directory of Lexington, Kentucky,* 1888, 146; *City Directory of Lexington, Kentucky,* 1890, 243.

40. Thompson, *Madam Belle Brezing,* 51.

41. Ibid.

42. Tanner, "Fifty Years Recollections of Lexington and Vicinity," 109.

43. "Petition of Citizens," *Lexington Daily Press,* January 12, 1889; Sparks, *Kentucky's Most Hated Man,* 156.

44. *Commonwealth of Kentucky v. Mike Foley,* November 26, 1886.

45. *Kentucky Leader,* June 16, 1889.

6. A Wealthy Benefactor

1. "Dealing with Unions," *Pittsburgh Dispatch,* December 16, 1891.

2. Malone, *Dictionary of American Biography,* 189–90.

3. "Belmont Track Is Flourishing," *Philadelphia Inquirer,* August 13, 1905;

"George Singerly Has Passed Away," *Philadelphia Inquirer*, March 22, 1902; "Roland's Racing Review," *Chicago Daily Inter Ocean*, May 18, 1890.

4. *Philadelphia Inquirer*, March 22, 1902.

5. *Lexington Morning Herald*, December 13, 1896. Ash Grove Farm later became the property of Colonel E. R. Bradley, four-time winner of the Kentucky Derby, who changed the name to Idle Hour Farm.

6. Ibid; "Among the Kentucky Breeders," *Wallace's Monthly*, December 1886, 732–34.

7. "Revival of Racing at the North," *Spirit of the Times*, September 3, 1859, 355; Adelman, *A Sporting Time*, 78.

8. McCarr, *The Kentucky Harness Horse*, 18–21.

9. Ibid., 18.

10. Leerhsen, *Crazy Good*, 7–10.

11. McCarr, *The Kentucky Harness Horse*, 7–10, 29.

12. Ibid., 26–31.

13. Ibid., 36–41.

14. "Mambrino in Kentucky," *Spirit of the Times*, May 1, 1880, 298.

15. "Forest Park Training and Stud Farm," *Turf, Field and Farm*, February 5, 1879, 82; McCarr, *The Kentucky Harness Horse*, 23.

16. "Forest Park Training and Stud Farm," 82.

17. Mackay-Smith, *The Race Horses of America*, 300.

18. McCarr, *The Kentucky Harness Horse*, 23.

19. "Belmont Track Is Flourishing."

20. Leerhsen, *Crazy Good*, 8.

21. "Belmont's Big Boom," *Philadelphia Inquirer*, May 3, 1889; "Belmont's Election," *Philadelphia Inquirer*, May 3, 1895; *Philadelphia Inquirer*, 1889.

22. *Horse Review*, March 8, 1898, 229; "Turf Topics," *Idaho Statesman*, March 8, 1893.

23. "The Racing Season Opens at Elkton," *Philadelphia Inquirer*, October 20, 1895; "Mr. Cleveland with Mr. Singerly," *Philadelphia Patriot*, September 24, 1888; "The President's Sunday," *New York Times*, September 24, 1888; "The *Restless* Launched," *Philadelphia Inquirer*, April 21, 1887; "The President Goes Yachting," *Philadelphia Patriot*, July 11, 1887.

24. "Sporting Generalities," *Cleveland Leader*, November 17, 1887; "Track and Trade Notes," *Philadelphia Inquirer*, May 3, 1896; "Track and Stable Talk," *Aberdeen (S. Dak.) Daily News*, January 17, 1888; "Kentucky and Her Horsemen," *Kentucky Stock Farm*, July 11, 1899, 7.

25. "Kentucky and Her Horsemen."

26. "Miss Belle's Angel," typed notes of Skeets Meadors, Thompson Papers, box 41, folder 21. Next to George Singerly's name, Buddy Thompson handwrote "error" and affixed his initials, B.T. See also Thompson, *Madam Belle Brezing*, 62.

27. Bowden, *Boise Penrose*, 99; Davenport, *Power and Glory*, 52–53.

7. Lexington's Exclusive Mansion for Men

1. Townsend, *The Most Orderly of Disorderly Houses*, 5.

2. Clark, *My Century in History*, 334, 343.

3. Ibid., 343, 344; Townsend, *The Most Orderly of Disorderly Houses*, 5–6.

4. Townsend, *The Most Orderly of Disorderly Houses*, 5–6.

5. J. B. Moore interview, Thompson Papers, box 41, folder 21; Thompson, *Madam Belle Brezing*, 64–65.

6. Thompson, *Madam Belle Brezing*, 99.

7. Sayre interview; R. L. Polk & Co., *Lexington City Guide, 1912–1913*, 443.

8. Shumsky, "Tacit Acceptance."

9. Bullough, *The History of Prostitution*, 194–95; Rosen, *The Lost Sisterhood*, 79.

10. Williams, "The Voice of Whiteness," 74. Williams argued that Louisville made a conscious decision to overlap its red-light district with sections of that city occupied by impoverished African Americans.

11. Letter to Governor S. B. Buckner (the name of person writing the letter is not decipherable), January 11, 1888, Thompson Papers, box 40, folder 20.

12. "Stamp for Special Tax," United States Internal Revenue, Received from Belle Brezing, $25 special tax on the business of Retail Liquor Dealer, 59 McGowen [*sic*] St., April 2, 1895, copy in possession of author.

13. Washburn, *Come into My Parlor*, 27.

14. Ibid., 23.

15. Ibid., 23–30, 83.

16. "W. E. D. Stokes Dies of Pneumonia at 73," *New York Times*, May 20, 1926.

17. "Mrs. Stokes's Negro Ball: How the New York Woman Entertains the Colored People on Her Kentucky Farm," *New York Times*, October 3, 1897, 3.

18. "Mrs. Stokes's Fast Horses," *New York Times*, October 16, 1896; "W. E. D. Stokes," *Horse Review*, May 26, 1926.

19. *Spirit of the Times*, January 1, 1887, 702.

20. "A Beautiful Kentucky Estate—Walnut Hall," *Illustrated Sporting News*, May 23, 1903, 11.

21. Blanche Patterson interview with Skeets Meadors, August 1941, Thompson Papers, box 41, folder 21.

22. Ibid.

23. Clara Sayre interview with Skeets Meadors, Thompson Papers, box 41, folder 21.

24. Ibid.

25. "Clem Beachey, Sr., Dead," *Horse Review*, May 2, 1917, 470.

26. "Weatherill Arrives with Twelve Horses," *Lexington Herald*, March 24, 1911.

27. Sayre interview with Meadors.

28. Ibid.

29. Featherstone interview.

30. Sayre interview with Meadors; "Empire of the Lucky," *Blood-Horse*, January 2, 1982, 60–63.

31. "News and Gossip of the Running Turf," *Brooklyn Eagle*, January 15, 1901, 14.

32. "Empire of the Lucky."

33. "Sketch of the Lexington Fire Department," *Lexington Morning Herald*, September 22, 1901.

34. "The Rush of an Engine to a Fire," undated clipping, Kaufman Papers, scrapbook, 2.

35. *Lexington Morning Herald*, September 22, 1901.

36. Moore interview; "Mass of Ruins," *Lexington Press-Transcript*, March 17, 1895.

37. "Mass of Ruins."

38. Ibid.

39. Thomas interview.

40. Townsend, *The Most Orderly of Disorderly Houses*, 3; Thompson, *Madam Belle Brezing*, 89–90. Thompson wrote that he heard this story from the late Phil Minor, a bookmaker in Lexington. Minor refused to name names because, according to Thompson, the two men who engaged in the fight came from families "still prominent in town."

41. Some accounts have Belle purchasing the bed at the Lexington Exposition in 1894. John Coyne, a bartender who knew her well, said Belle might have acquired the bedroom suite from Riley Grannan. John Coyne interview with Skeets Meadors, Thompson Papers, box 41, folder 21.

42. "A Trio of Famous Plungers," *Live Stock Record*, December 15, 1894, 372–73.

43. Hollingsworth, *The Great Ones*, 140–43; "He Was a Dead Game Sport," *Lexington Herald*, February 3, 1974.

44. John Coyne interview, Thompson Papers, box 41, folder 21.

45. "The Navarre to Be Sold," *Thoroughbred Record*, July 27, 1895, 46; C. Frank Dunn, "Blue Grass and Horse Feathers," *Lexington Herald*, July 16, 1933.

8. A Uniquely Powerful Woman in a Changing City

1. "A Futurity for Morello," *New York Times*, August 28, 1892.

2. Ibid.

3. "Meted Out Summary Punishments," *Cleveland Leader*, December 6, 1888; *Philadelphia Inquirer*, December 15, 1895.

4. "Horsedom Lost Great Driver in Van Ness," *Springfield (Ill.) Republican*, April 14, 1929.

5. "A Futurity for Morello."

6. Ibid.

7. Ibid.

8. "Will Morello Run?" *New Orleans Picayune*, May 2, 1893.

9. "Morello Can Start," *Chicago Daily Inter Ocean*, May 5, 1893.

10. "Frank Van Ness' Horses: They Became Dope Fiends and Refused to Run Consistently," *Philadelphia Inquirer*, December 26, 1893.

11. *Philadelphia Inquirer*, December 15, 1895.

12. *New York Times*, quoted in ibid.

13. "Turf and Track," *New York Times*, November 6, 1891; Keeneland, Deluxe Souvenir, 70.

14. Ibid.; Hollingsworth, *The Great Ones*, 270.

15. "Our City Fathers," Kaufman Papers, box 4; *Turf, Field and Farm*, February 28, 1896, 302; *Turf, Field and Farm*, February 21, 1896, 274.

16. Morelock, *Taking the Town*, 199.

17. Thomas interview, box 41, folder 21.

18. "Philadelphia Banks Fail," *New York Herald-Tribune*, December 24, 1897; "Half in Stock, Half in Cash," *Philadelphia Inquirer*, December 26, 1897.

19. "William M. Singerly Dead," *New York Times*, February 28, 1898.

20. "Geo. A. S. Singerly Dead," *Baltimore Sun*, March 22, 1902.

21. *Lexington Morning Herald*, October 9, 1897.

22. *Lexington Morning Herald*, October 10, 1897.

23. *Lexington Morning Herald*, October 7, 1897.

24. *Kentucky Leader*, February 22, 1891, Kaufman Papers.

25. Brock, *A History of the Woman's Club of Central Kentucky*, 17.

26. Ibid., 17–18.

27. Womack, "The Urban Development of Lexington, 1870–1910," 17; Coleman, *The Squire's Sketches of Lexington*, 62; *Kentucky Leader*, April 9, 1890.

28. "City Siftings," *Lexington Morning Herald*, March 4, 1896; "Unconscious and Bleeding," *Lexington Morning Herald*, March 3, 1896; *Kentucky Leader*, April 20, 1890; "Mr. Treacy's Session," *Kentucky Leader*, October 10, 1890.

29. "Belt Land Sale," *Kentucky Leader*, April 7, 1890.

30. Hollingsworth, *The Wizard of the Turf*, 11. See also Bowen, *Legacies of the Turf*, 25–35.

31. Hollingsworth, *The Wizard of the Turf*, 12–14.

32. Ibid., 23, 29.

33. Pryor, *Doctor Pryor*, 90.

34. Ibid., 91.

9. Crackdown on Vice

1. Cherie Suchy, "Legacy of the Land," *Thoroughbred Record,* January 7, 1981, 48–51.

2. Ibid., 49; Maryjean Wall, "History Repeating," *Lexington Herald-Leader,* September 11, 2002.

3. Sergent, "The Pastime of Millions."

4. Ibid.

5. Nicholson, *The Kentucky Derby,* 15; Sergent, "The Pastime of Millions," 107–8.

6. "The Week," *Illustrated Sporting News,* July 23, 1904.

7. Ibid., 164.

8. Dr. C. A. Nevitt interview by Skeets Meadors, July 15, 1941, Thompson Papers, box 40, folder 2; James Tandy Ellis to Tom R. Underwood, August 14, 1940, Thompson Papers, box 40, folder 4. Underwood was editor of the *Lexington Herald.*

9. Thomas interview.

10. Sayre interview with Meadors.

11. Coyne interview.

12. Chinn interview.

13. Ibid.

14. "As related from some of Lexington's oldtimers," Thompson Papers, box 40, folder 3.

15. *Horse Review,* October 8, 1913; *Horse Review,* November 5, 1913, 1396.

16. Linda Ashley to Buddy Thompson, June 1, 1983, and June 14, 1983, Thompson Papers, box 41, folder 8. Ashley appears to be a genealogist from Rochester, Michigan, who engaged in considerable effort tracking down Belle's daughter for Thompson. Ashley did some amazing sleuthing, for Daisy May spent nearly all her life in institutions. During the early 1980s, Ashley obtained some information from the Sisters of the Good Shepherd in Dearborn Heights, Michigan, which filled gaps in the story of Belle's only child. She explained a delay in finding records of the daughter due to the name changes and the terrible writing of the nun who kept records of the girls.

17. Fayette Grand Jury report to Fayette Circuit Court, May 15, 1908, in possession of author.

18. Rosen, *The Lost Sisterhood,* xii. Rosen identifies a national antivice campaign emerging between 1900 and 1918.

19. Thompson, *Madam Belle Brezing,* 79.

20. "If They Can Be Closed Why Are They Not Closed?" *Lexington Herald,* September 10, 1913.

21. "Mass Meeting Raises Considerable Interest," *Lexington Herald,* December 5, 1913.

22. Niles Papers, 82M9, box 71, folder 7.

23. Ibid.; Lee told Thompson that Belle's house had a silver door knocker (Lee interview).

24. Niles Papers, 82M9, box 71, folder 7.

25. Ibid.

26. Grand Jury Report to Fayette Circuit Court, July 24, 1911, copy in author's possession; "Grand Jury Advises Obliteration of the Red Light District," *Lexington Herald,* November 8, 1913.

27. The grand jury report is reprinted in full in "Grand Jury Advises Obliteration of the Red Light District."

28. "14-Year-Old Girl," *Lexington Leader,* January 9, 1907.

29. "Robbed," *Lexington Morning Herald,* April 17, 1897; "Afraid to Probe for Bullet in Brain," *Lexington Herald,* January 12, 1911; "Savage's Assailant Captured," *Lexington Herald,* January 12, 1911; "Vaughn Found Guilty of Murdering Wife," *Lexington Herald,* January 14, 1911.

30. Thompson, *Madam Belle Brezing,* 101–2.

31. Ibid.

32. "Vice Commission for Lexington Requested," *Lexington Herald,* November 4, 1914.

33. "Vice Report Is Filed with Commissioners," *Lexington Herald,* June 15, 1915.

34. "Grand Jury Advises Obliteration of the Red Light District."

10. A Growing Moral Menace

1. Linda Ashley to Buddy Thompson, June 14, 1983.

2. *Lexington Fire Department Commemorative Book,* 16.

3. Bowen, *Legacies of the Turf,* 63–72.

4. Ibid, 105–14.

5. Tracy Gantz, "Kinzea Stone," *Blood-Horse,* April 26, 1980, 2236–44.

6. Ambrose, *The Lexington Motor Car,* 2, 51–62.

7. Ibid.

8. Lowry and White, *A Century of Speed: The Red Mile,* 25.

9. Robertson and Farley, *Hoofprints of the Century,* 127; "Superb Success Attends Restoration of Racing at Famous Association Track," *Lexington Herald,* May 4, 1905.

10. "Probability of a Race Meeting," *Kentucky Farmer and Breeder,* February 1, 1906, 8.

11. Ibid.; John Coyne interview with Skeets Meadors, Thompson Papers, box 41, folder 6.

12. "Lexington's Spring Race Meeting Opens Next Monday," *Kentucky Farmer and Breeder,* April 20, 1906, 5; "A Souvenir from the Kentucky Association," 28.

13. "Gratification at Racing Commission," *Kentucky Farmer and Breeder,* March 30, 1906, 11.

14. "Major Louis Beard to Manage Farm for Harry Payne Whitney," *Lexington Leader,* October 25, 1925, contains the information that Berryman previously had managed Harry Payne's breeding interests in Lexington.

15. Bolus, *Run for the Roses,* 27.

16. "Vice Report Is Filed with Commissioners."

17. Fayette Grand Jury Report, November 13, 1915, copy in possession of the author.

18. "Measures to Close Vice District Are Passed by 4 Votes," *Lexington Herald,* November 27, 1915.

19. Ibid.

20. Ibid.

21. "Police Will Enforce Anti-Vice Ordinances," *Lexington Herald,* November 28, 1915.

22. "Measures Closing Vice District are Effective Today," *Lexington Herald,* November 29, 1915.

23. Ibid.

24. "No Immediate Move to Enforce Vice Ordinances," *Lexington Herald,* November 30, 1915.

25. "Restricted District in Lexington Passes," *Lexington Herald,* December 22, 1915.

26. "Restricted District Is Thing of the Past," *Lexington Herald,* January 16, 1916.

27. "William Mabon," *Lexington Leader,* February 17, 1917, quoted in Thompson, *Madam Belle Brezing,* 117.

28. Thompson, *Madam Belle Brezing,* 122.

29. *Lexington Leader,* October 23, 1917.

30. Ibid.

31. Ibid.

11. The Passing of a Legend

1. The *Morning Transcript* to Belle Brezing, 194 North Upper Street, Invoice, January 2, 1889, to April 22, 1889, Thompson Papers, box 38, folder 4.

2. Palmer, *This Was Racing,* 43.

3. Margaret Egbert interview with Burton Milward, Thompson Papers, box 40, folder 5.

4. Ibid.

5. Ibid.

6. Ibid.

7. Thomas interview, box 41, folder 6; card file from Calvary Cemetery, Thompson Papers, box 40, folder 8.

8. Thompson, *Madam Belle Brezing*, 173.

9. Bob Morgan, interview with author, Lexington, February 20, 2014.

10. Thompson, *Madam Belle Brezing*, 141.

11. Ibid., 142.

12. Ibid., 142–43; card file from Calvary Cemetery, Thompson Papers, box 40, folder 8, and box 41, folder 21. Thompson noted that the cemetery informational card on Belle is filed as Belle McM Kenny, or Kenney. McM stands for McMeekin. Thompson Papers, box 40, folder 16.

13. Rodgers Baker interview by Burton Milward, September 1971, Thompson Papers, box 40, folder 5; "In the Matter of the Estate of Belle Brezing, Deceased," July 2, 1941, book 41, 94.

14. "Bell Breazing Dead," *Lexington Leader,* August 12, 1940.

15. "End Comes to Belle Breazing," *Lexington Herald,* August 13, 1940; *Highlights and Shadows,* in-house publication of the *Louisville Courier-Journal,* cited in Thompson, *Madam Belle Brezing,* 146.

16. "End Comes to Belle Breazing."

17. Ibid.

18. Ibid.; "Milestones," *Time,* August 26, 1940.

19. "Milestones."

20. Graves, *To My Footloose Correspondents.*

21. Thompson, *Madam Belle Brezing,* 145; "Public Auction," advertisement in *Lexington Leader,* August 21, 1940; Appraisal, Belle Brezing Estate, Fayette County Court, August 16, 1940, Inventory and Appraisement Book, 14, 386–87.

22. Thompson, *Madam Belle Brezing,* 161–63.

23. Ibid., 165–66.

24. State of Michigan, in the Probate Court for the County of Wayne, in the Matter of the Estate of Daisy Kenney, no. 95705, Thompson Papers, box 41, folder 8; State of Michigan, the Probate Court for the County of Wayne, Physician's Certificate (Edward Mooney), in the Matter of Daisy Kenney, August 23, 1922, Thompson Papers, box 41, folder 8; State of Michigan, the Probate Court for the County of Wayne, Physician's Certificate (Harriet L. Hawkins), in the Matter of Daisy Kenney, August 23, 1922, Thompson Papers, box 41, folder 8.

25. State of Michigan in the Probate Court for the County of Wayne, in the Matter of the Estate of Daisy Kenney, no. 95,705, deposition of Dr. C. A. Nevitt, Thompson Papers, box 41, folder 8; Thompson, *Madam Belle Brezing,* 167.

26. Thompson, *Madam Belle Brezing,* 169–70.

27. Ibid., 168.

28. "In the Matter of Belle Brezing, Deceased, First and Final Settlement," Fayette County Court, Inventory and Appraisement, book 41, 93–95.

29. Ibid.

30. Thompson, *Madam Belle Brezing,* 174–75; "Flora Hudson, Who Operated Old Hudson Hotel, Dies at 89," *Lexington Herald-Leader,* May 8, 1987.

31. "News Release: Arson Division, Lexington Metro Fire Department (Major Bob Works) 12-17-73," quoted in Thompson, *Madam Belle Brezing,* 175–76.

32. Thompson, *Madam Belle Brezing,* 178, 176–77.

33. Ibid., 176–77.

34. Tom Eblen, "A Famous Belle's Bed Goes on Sale," *Atlanta Constitution,* September 11, 1987; "Flora Hudson, Who Operated Old Hudson Hotel, Dies at 89"; "Brezing's Bed Sold for $13,230 at Estate Auction," *Lexington Herald-Leader,* September 21, 1987.

35. Thompson, *Madam Belle Brezing,* 180.

Epilogue

1. Walker, *Margaret Mitchell and John Marsh.*

2. Ibid., 49. The interview with Francesca Marsh is cited in 527n8.

3. Edwards, *Road to Tara,* 139; Walker, *Margaret Mitchell and John Marsh,* 317, 319. Francesca Marsh is cited as the source in 538n15.

4. Thompson, *Madam Belle Brezing,* 179.

Bibliography

Primary Sources

Birds Eye View of Lexington, Ky. (map), 1871. Kentucky Room, Lexington Public Library Central Branch.

Brezing, Sarah vs. George Brezing. Fayette County Circuit Court, Civil Case Files, box 168, Kentucky Department for Libraries and Archives, Frankfort.

Brock, Loretta Gilliam. *A History of the Woman's Club of Central Kentucky, 1894–1994.* Lexington: Woman's Club of Central Kentucky, 1996.

City Directory of Lexington, Kentucky. Lexington: Prather & Snyder, 1888.

City Directory of Lexington, Kentucky. Lexington: J. "Hub" Prather, 1890.

City Directory of Lexington, Kentucky, 1887. Chattanooga, Tenn.: Norwood, Connelly, 1887.

Coleman, J. Winston, Jr. *Belle Breezing: A Famous Lexington Bawd.* Lexington: Winburn, 1980.

———. *Lexington during the Civil War.* Lexington: Henry Clay, 1968.

———. *The Squire's Sketches of Lexington.* Lexington: Henry Clay, 1972.

Commonwealth of Kentucky v. Belle Brezing, December 12, 1882. Fayette County Indictments, box 8, drawers 70–72, Kentucky Department for Libraries and Archives, Frankfort.

Commonwealth of Kentucky v. Belle Brezing, November 26, 1866. Fayette County Indictments, box 11, drawers 95–97, Kentucky Department for Libraries and Archives, Frankfort.

Commonwealth of Kentucky v. James Cox, November 29, 1886. Fayette County Indictments, box 11, drawers 98–100, Kentucky Department for Libraries and Archives, Frankfort.

Commonwealth of Kentucky v. Mike Foley, November 26, 1886. Fayette County Indictments, box 11, drawers 95–97, Kentucky Department for Libraries and Archives, Frankfort.

Crickmore, H. G., ed. *Racing Calendars, 1861–1865.* New York: W. D Whitney, 1901.

Fayette County Deed Books 68, 76, 82, 103. Office of Fayette County Clerk, Lexington.

Fayette County Grand Jury Reports, 1908, 1911, 1915. Copies in possession of author.

Fayette County Indictments, 1882, 1886. Kentucky Department for Libraries, Frankfort.

Fayette County Inventory and Appraisement Book, 1940. Office of Fayette County Clerk, Lexington.

Fayette County Mortgage Books, 7, 8, 10, 11, 12, 13. Office of Fayette County Clerk, Lexington.

Fayette County Tax Assessment Book, 1890. Kentucky Department for Libraries and Archives, Frankfort.

Graves, Joe. *To My Footloose Correspondents.* Lexington: privately printed, 1969.

Hellrigle, R. C., & Co. *Lexington City Directory and Gazetteer Cincinnati Southern Railway, 1877–8.* Lexington: R. C. Hellrigle, 1877.

Kaufman, Moses, Papers. Special Collections, University of Kentucky Libraries, Lexington.

Keeneland, Deluxe Souvenir. Lexington: C. T. Dearing, 1936.

Lexington Fire Department Commemorative Book, 1790–1993. Lexington: Lexington Fire Department, 1994.

Mackay-Smith, Alexander. *The Race Horses of America, 1832–1872: Portraits and Other Paintings by Edward Troye.* Saratoga Springs, N.Y.: National Museum of Racing, 1981.

Malone, Dumas, ed. *Dictionary of American Biography.* New York: Charles Scribner's Sons, 1936.

McMeekin, William S., and Sallie Brezing, May 18, 1870, Kentucky Marriages, 1785–1979. Louisville, Jefferson County, Kentucky, familysearch. org, microfilm 482711.

Niles, John Jacob, Papers. Special Collections, University of Kentucky Libraries, Lexington.

Polk, R. L., & Co. *Lexington City Guide, 1912–1913.* Chicago: R. L. Polk, n.d.

Prather's Lexington City Directory for 1875 and 1876. Lexington: Jas. H. Prather, 1876.

Pryor, J. W. *Doctor Pryor.* Cynthiana, Ky.: Jacobson, 1943.

Ranck, George Washington. *A Review of Lexington, Kentucky, as She Is.* New York: John Lethem, 1886.

Sayers, Warner. *Lexington Club.* Lexington: privately printed, 1937.

Smith, John David, ed. *Window on the War: Frances Dallam Peter's Lexington Civil War Diary.* Lexington: Lexington-Fayette County Historic Commission, 1976.

"A Souvenir from the Kentucky Association." N.p., 1926.

Tanner, Joseph M. "Fifty Years Recollections of Lexington and Vicinity, Its People and Institutions." Joseph M. Tanner Papers, Special Collections, University of Kentucky Libraries, Lexington.

Thompson, E. I. "Buddy," Papers. Special Collections, University of Kentucky Libraries, Lexington.

Topographical Map, Lexington West, Ky., 1965, Kentucky Geological Survey. Kentucky Room, Lexington Public Library.

Townsend, William H. *The Most Orderly of Disorderly Houses.* Lexington: privately printed, 1966.

Townsend and Company's Lexington Directory for 1883–1884. Chattanooga, Tenn.: Connelly, n.d.

United States Federal Census, 1880. Lexington: Williams, 1881.

Williams' Lexington City Directory for 1881–82. Lexington: Williams, 1881.

Womack, Jay. "The Urban Development of Lexington, 1870–1910." Manuscript, 1973. Special Collections, Transylvania University.

Secondary Sources

Adelman, Melvin L. *A Sporting Time: New York City and the Rise of Modern Athletics, 1820–70.* Urbana: University of Illinois Press, 1986.

Ambrose, William M. *The Lexington Motor Car: Bred in Old Kentucky.* Lexington: Limestone Press of Kentucky, 2007.

Bolin, James Duane. *Bossism and Reform in a Southern City: Lexington, Kentucky, 1880–1940.* Lexington: University Press of Kentucky, 2000.

Bolus, Jim. *Run for the Roses: 100 Years at the Kentucky Derby.* New York: Hawthorn Books, 1974.

Bowden, Robert Douglas. *Boise Penrose, Symbol of an Era.* New York: Greenberg, 1937.

Bowen, Edward L. *Legacies of the Turf: A Century of Great Thoroughbred Breeders.* Vol. 1. Lexington: Eclipse, 2003.

Bullough, Vern L. *The History of Prostitution.* New Hyde Park, N.Y.: University Books, 1964.

Clark, Thomas D. *My Century in History: Memoirs.* Lexington: University Press of Kentucky, 2006.

Davenport, Walter. *Power and Glory: The Life of Boise Penrose.* New York: G. P. Putnam's Sons, 1931.

Dippie, Brian W., ed. *Nomad: George A. Custer in "Turf, Field and Farm."* Austin: University of Texas Press, 1980.

Edwards, Anne. *Road to Tara: The Life of Margaret Mitchell.* New Haven, Conn.: Ticknor & Fields, 1983.

Hollingsworth, Kent. *The Great Ones.* Lexington: Blood Horse, 1970.

———. *The Wizard of the Turf: John E. Madden of Hamburg Place*. Lexington: privately printed, 1965.

Hollingsworth, Randolph. *Lexington, Queen of the Bluegrass*. Charleston: Arcadia, 2004.

Kleber, John E., ed. *The Kentucky Encyclopedia*. Lexington: University Press of Kentucky, 1992.

Leerhsen, Charles. *Crazy Good: The True Story of Dan Patch, the Most Famous Horse in America*. New York: Simon & Schuster, 2008.

Lowry, Biff, and Tom White. *A Century of Speed: The Red Mile, 1976–2003*. 2nd ed. Lexington: Post Printing, 2003.

McCarr, Ken. *The Kentucky Harness Horse*. Lexington: University Press of Kentucky, 1978.

Morelock, Kolan Thomas. *Taking the Town: Collegiate and Community Culture in the Bluegrass, 1880–1917*. Lexington: University Press of Kentucky, 2008.

Musto, David F. *The American Disease: Origins of Narcotic Control*. Oxford: Oxford University Press, 1973.

Nicholson, James C. *The Kentucky Derby: How the Run for the Roses Became America's Premier Sporting Event*. Lexington: University Press of Kentucky, 2012.

Palmer, Joe M. *This Was Racing*. Edited by Red Smith. Lexington: Henry Clay, 1973.

Ramage, James A. *Rebel Raider: The Life of General John Hunt Morgan*. Lexington: University Press of Kentucky, 1986.

Robertson, William H. P. *The History of Thoroughbred Racing in America*. New York: Bonanza Books, 1964.

Robertson, William H. P., and Dan Farley, eds. *Hoofprints of the Century*. Lexington: Thoroughbred Record, 1975.

Rosen, Ruth. *The Lost Sisterhood: Prostitution in America, 1900–1918*. Baltimore: Johns Hopkins University Press, 1982.

Rosenberg, Charles E. *The Care of Strangers: The Rise of America's Hospital System*. New York: Basic Books, 1987.

Sergent, Amber Fogle. "The Pastime of Millions: James Ben Ali Haggin's Elmendorf Farm and the Commercialization of Animal Breeding, 1897–1920." Ph.D. diss., University of Kentucky, 2012.

Shumsky, Neil Larry. "Tacit Acceptance: Respectable Americans and Segregated Prostitution, 1870–1910." *Journal of Social History* 19, no. 4 (1986): 665–79.

Sparks, John. *Kentucky's Most Hated Man: Charles Chilton Moore and the Bluegrass Blade*. Nicholasville, Ky.: Wind, 2009.

Thompson, E. I. *Madam Belle Brezing*. Lexington: Buggy Whip, 1983.

Walker, Marianne. *Margaret Mitchell and John Marsh: The Love Story behind "Gone with the Wind."* Atlanta: Peachtree, 1993.

Bibliography

Wall, Maryjean. *How Kentucky Became Southern: A Tale of Outlaws, Horse Thieves, Gamblers, and Breeders.* Lexington: University Press of Kentucky, 2010.

Walzer, Judith Leavitt, and Ronald L. Numbers, eds. *Sickness and Health in America.* 3rd ed. Madison: University of Wisconsin Press, 1985.

Washburn, Charles. *Come into My Parlor.* New York: Arno, 1974.

Williams, Kathie E. "The Voice of Whiteness: Race, Sexuality, and the Language of Segregation." Ph.D. diss., University of Kentucky, 2001.

Index

Green Hills, 113
Grinstead, James A., 17, 47

Haggin, James Ben Ali, 49, 53, 88, 113–16, 122, 125, 129, 131, 133
Hagyard, Ed, 118
Hall, Rebecca, 144
Halleck, Henry Wager, 14
Halley, Samuel H., 125
Hamburg (horse), 110
Hamburg Place, 110
Hancock, Arthur, 129
Hancock, Richard Johnson, 129
Han d'Or (horse), 68
Hanover (horse), 68
Happy Medium (horse), 74
Harkness, Lamon, 88, 130
Harkness, S. V., 88
Harrison Narcotic Act, 116
Harrison School, 19
Harrison, Mrs. A. M., 125
Harrison, William Henry, 51
Harry Wilkes (horse), 101
Harvey, Debbie, 124
Hayward, William "Papa Bill," 101–2
Heatherington, James R., 19–20
Henry Clay Hotel, 53
Henry of Navarre (horse), 96
Herndon, James, 143
heroin, 43
Herr, Levi, 74–75
Herr Park, 128
Hill, Jennie, 45–46, 50–52, 62, 133
Hill (red-light district), 4, 85, 118–19, 127, 135–38
Hindoo (horse), 49, 133
hog pens in city, 40
Hoskins, George, 148
House of the Good Shepherd, 119
House of Mercy, 135

Hudson, Flora, 149, 151
Hughes, Pearl, 6–7, 141, 143–44
Hughes, Tandy, 61
Hull House, 125
Hunt, George R., 138
Hunt, Mrs. George R., 125
Hurst, F. M., 59
Hurst, George, 114
Hussey, John, 118
Hutchinson, E. L., 59

Idle Hour Farm, 129–30
Irvine, Mollie, 118

Jackson, Andrew, 51
James Pepper distillery, 23, 125
Jaubert, Gus, 38
Jay-Eye-See (horse), 72
Jockey Club, 99–100
Jordan, Joe, viii, 154
Josie B. (horse), 87

Kalakahua (king of Hawaii), 74
Keene, James R., 88
Keeneland, 143
Kelly, H. P., 109
Kenney, Daisy May, 34–35, 39, 61, 119, 127, 145, 147–49
Kenney, James, 29, 31, 33
Kentucky Association track: Aristides vs. Ten Broeck, 103; chicanery at, 7; Civil War, 16–17; closing of from 1898 to 1905, 73, 103; closing of in 1933, 143; connections to Phoenix Hotel, 37; hill obscures sightlines, 47; improvements to, 46; Man o' War's farewell, 141; proximity to red-light district, 3; race weeks in Lexington, 46–47; trotting meet at, 47

Topics in Kentucky History

James C. Klotter, Series Editor

Books in the Series

The Family Legacy of Henry Clay: In the Shadow of a Kentucky Patriarch
Lindsey Apple

George Keats of Kentucky: A Life
Lawrence M. Crutcher

A History of Education in Kentucky
William E. Ellis

Madeline McDowell Breckinridge and the Battle for a New South
Melba Porter Hay

Henry Watterson and the New South: The Politics of Empire, Free Trade, and Globalization
Daniel S. Margolies

Murder and Madness: The Myth of the Kentucky Tragedy
Matthew G. Schoenbachler

How Kentucky Became Southern: A Tale of Outlaws, Horse Thieves, Gamblers, and Breeders
Maryjean Wall

Madam Belle: Sex, Money, and Influence in a Southern Brothel
Maryjean Wall

CPSIA information can be obtained at www.ICGtesting.com
Printed in the USA
BVOW04*0038181214

378700BV00001B/1/P